# Women Included

## A Book of Services and Prayers

### The St Hilda Community

First published in Great Britain
1991
SPCK
Holy Trinity Church
Marylebone Road
London NW1 4DU

British Library Cataloguing in
Publication Data
Women included.
1. Christianity. Women
I. St Hilda Community
262.15

ISBN 0-281-04531-3

Printed in Great Britain by
Dotesios Limited, Trowbridge
Typeset by Rowland
Phototypesetting Limited,
Bury St Edmunds, Suffolk

**In Memory of Jim**

Many members of St Hilda's were shocked when James Tatham – Jim – died suddenly in July. He had been complaining of feeling ill for some weeks, and not long before his death, at his request, we had prayed specially for him at a service, gathering round him and gently placing our hands on his shoulders and head. Jim, a roadsweeper, belonged to the old East End, and had grown up spiritually in the East End Anglo-Catholic tradition. Interestingly, he seemed to find no difficulty in seeing Suzanne Fageol and other women priests as part of the succession of remarkable 'fathers' he had known in his youth. For a while he used to refer to Suzanne as 'Father'; whether he was teasing us or not we were never quite sure! He came almost every week to St Hilda's, a huge presence, at first very silent, who appreciated the freedom and informality of our style (and often slipped out for a cigarette or a cup of tea when our conversations or our prayers bored him!). Jim had had a hard life, which made him very sensitive to the suffering of others, and we have not forgotten the love and pain with which he lit a candle 'for those in mental hospitals, particularly any undergoing shock treatment'. He used to pray at home for any of us with particular troubles, and often made a point of asking us later about the welfare of those he had prayed for. What remains with us is a sense of his great goodness and love. We miss him more than we can say.

July, 1990

# Women Included

# Contents

**ix**    Acknowledgements

**Part One**

**5**    Introduction: A 'Non-Sexist' Community *Monica Furlong*
**16**    Celebrating Experience *Suzanne Fageol*
**27**    The Nitty-Gritty: Organisation and Practicalities *Pat Willmitt*
**32**    Finding Our Balance: Dance at St Hilda's *Lillalou Hughes*

**Part Two**

**37**    Introducing a Service
**38**    Opening Acclamations
**41**    The Gloria
**43**    Collects
**46**    Canticles
**48**    Confessions of Faith
**52**    Discussion
**53**    Intercessions
**55**    Litany
**57**    Forms of Confession
**60**    Absolution
**61**    The Peace
**62**    The Offertory
**63**    Prayer of Jesus
**64**    Agape
**66**    The Eucharist
**80**    Post Communion
**81**    Blessing
**82**    Palm Sunday Rite
**83**    Music
**86**    Silent Eucharist
**89**    Final Prayer
**91**    Index of First Lines

## Acknowledge-ments

The following members of the St Hilda Community contributed to this book: Ann Arthur, Elsie Baker, Angela Barkes, Angela Berners-Wilson, Andrew Blackburn, Jan Chappell, Ann Clarke, Caroline Davis, Brenda Denvir, Erica Dunmow, Nigel Dunn, Suzanne Fageol, Peter Francis, Monica Furlong, Caroline Gilbert, Julie Hare, Lesley Hitchens, Lillalou Hughes, Jenny Hulin, Edna Jamieson, Keith Jenkins, David and Nerissa Jones, Judith Kemp, Peter Kettle, Jenny King, Jackie Long, Cecelia Lynch, Ingrid Masterson, Dorothea McEwan, Janet Morley, Mary Newby, Margaret Orr Deas, Mark Parker, Sue Parks, Mark Polglase, John and Mary Quenby, Bridget Rees, Claire Robson, Sally Rogers, Barbara Ross, Katharine Rumens, Ali Rusbridge, Andrew Sillett, Nicola Slee, James Tatham, Liz Waller, Hannah Ward, Anthea Williams, Pat Willmitt, Joy Wotton, Joyce Yarrow, Deborah Zachary, and others who have shared in our worship from time to time.

The St Hilda Community would like to thank the following for permission to reproduce copyright material:

The Congregation of Abraxas, First Unitarian Church of Berkeley CA, for 'The feast is ended, depart in peace'.

David Adam for 'Glory in all my seeing', 'From the flowing of the tide to its ebbing' and 'God of love and tenderness' from *Tides and Seasons* (Triangle/SPCK 1989).

Ann Arthur for 'Today we share bread and wine together' and 'Let us give thanks'.

The Ashram Community Trust for 'I light the candle, the light shines out' and 'As women break bread' from *Community Worship* (Ashram Community Trust).

# Acknowledgements

Jim Cotter for 'Be in love with life' and 'The blessing of God' from *Prayer at Night* (Cairns Publications, 4th edition, 1988), 'O God I seek you while you may be found' from *Prayer in the Morning* (Cairns Publications, 2nd edition, 1990) and 'Beloved, our Father and Mother' from *Healing – more or less* (Cairns Publications 1987).

Darton Longman and Todd for 'Peace and love are always alive in us' from *Enfolded in Love: Daily Readings with Julian of Norwich* (Darton Longman and Todd 1980).

Brenda Denvir for 'We believe in the presence of God in the world'.

F. Gerald Downing for 'Rage, Wisdom, and our lives inflame' (*Chrysalis*, MOW, June 1987).

Erica Dunmow for 'Sisters and brothers of the Community of St Hilda'.

Suzanne Fageol for the Silent Eucharist.

Monica Furlong for 'We adore the glory and the truth that is God', 'Jesus, who was lost and found in the garden', 'O God, we bring you our failure', 'We hold up our smallness to your greatness', 'God, who cares for us', 'O God, our Father and Mother' and 'Those who work for change suffer resistance'.

Edwina Gateley for 'Be silent, Be still' and 'Into your hands, Lord' from *Psalms of a Laywoman* (Claretian Publications 1981).

Beth Hamilton for 'Once upon a time' from 'The Journey' (included in *Womanguides*, ed. Rosemary Radford Ruether, Beacon Press, Boston, 1985).

Carter Heyward for 'In the beginning was God'.

Lillalou Hughes for compiling 'The bread we bring'.

The Iona Community for 'The Drama of Creation' and 'The Drama of the Incarnation'.

Keith Jenkins for 'Today we share bread and wine together' and 'Let us give thanks'.

Peter Kettle for 'This, the springtime of the year', the second verse of 'Be gentle when you touch bread' and 'Broken for us'.

Ann Lewin for 'Flame-dancing Spirit' from *By the Way* (1990).

Lillenas Publishing Company/Thankyou Music for 'You shall go out with joy' by Stuart Dauermann © 1975.

George MacLeod for 'Let thy Resurrection light radiate all our worship' from *The Whole Earth Shall Cry Glory* (Wild Goose Publications 1985).

Janet Morley for 'God our vision', 'O God our deliverer you cast down the mighty', 'Christ our healer', 'Spirit of integrity', 'Spirit of truth whom the world can never grasp', 'God our deliverer, whose approaching birth', 'God our mother', 'O God, the power of the powerless', 'For the darkness of waiting', 'May the God who dances in creation', 'Blessed is our brother Jesus' and 'May Holy Wisdom' from *All Desires Known* (WIT/MOW 1988) and also for 'God of the outsider'.

The NCCC, USA, for 'Keeper and Companion of us all' from the study on 'The Community of Women and Men in the Church' and Commission on Faith and Order (included in *No Longer Strangers*, WCC Publications 1983).

The National Christian Education Council for 'We do not understand, eternal God' from *Prayers for the Church Community* compiled by Roy Chapman and Donald Hilton (NCEC).

Oxford Women's Liturgy for 'God of justice and peace, you stand with those who are poor'.

R. G. Parsons c/o the Canterbury Press for 'O living bread from heaven'.

Penguin Books for an extract from *Bede: A History of the English Church and People*, trans. Leo Sherley-Price, © 1955, 1968 (Penguin Classics, revised edition, 1968).

Elizabeth Rice for 'The living God, the living, moving Spirit of God' (included in *No Longer Strangers*, WCC Publications 1983).

Nicola Slee for 'We believe in God – Maker, Redeemer and Sustainer of Life'.

Ateliers et Presses de Taizé for 'Ubi caritas et amor', 'Jubilate Deo', 'O Lord, hear my prayer' and 'Bless the Lord, my soul'.

Elsa Tamez for 'Come let us celebrate the supper of Jesus'.

Commission on Common Worship, Unitarian Universalist Association for 'From the fragmented world of our everyday lives' (included in *Leading Congregations in Worship – A Guide*).

Rachel C. Wahlberg for 'We believe in God who created women and men' (included in *No Longer Strangers*, WCC Publications 1983).

Judith Walker-Riggs for 'May the power and the mystery go before us' (included in *Echoes*, Unitarian Worship Sub-committee 1982).

Liz Waller for 'Glory be to you, Ground of all Being' and 'I deny God's gifts in me'.

Pat Willmitt for 'We need your forgiveness, merciful God'.

Lois M. Wilson for 'The blessing of the God of Sarah and Hagar, as of Abraham'.

Lala Winkley for 'God, lover of us all, most holy one'.

Miriam Therese Winter for 'In the beginning, in the very beginning' and 'I will pour clean water upon you' from *WomanPrayer, WomanSong* (Meyer-Stone Books).

and from traditional sources:

'Thanks be to God that we have risen this day' (Alexander Carmichael, *Carmina Gadelica*), and 'Now may every living being' (Sakyamuni Buddha).

The Community has made every effort to identify copyright holders and to obtain their permission, but would be glad to hear of any inadvertent errors or omissions.

# Part One

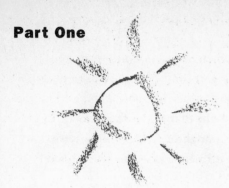

The life of Christ's servant Abbess Hilda, whom all her acquaintance called Mother because of her wonderful devotion and grace . . . was the fulfilment of a dream which her mother had when Hilda was an infant, during the time that her husband was living in banishment, where he died of poison. In this dream she fancied that he was suddenly taken away, and although she searched everywhere she could find no trace of him. When all her efforts had failed, she discovered a most valuable jewel under her garments; and as she looked closely, it emitted such a brilliant light that all Britain was lit by its splendour. This dream was fulfilled in her daughter, whose life afforded a shining example not only to herself but to all who wished to live a good life. . . .

Bede, *A History of the English Church and People.*

O GOD our vision,
in our mother's womb
you formed us for your glory.
As your servant Hilda
shone like a jewel in the church
may we now delight to claim her gifts
of judgment and inspiration
reflected in the women of this age,
through Jesus Christ, Amen.

Collect for St Hilda's Day
(November 17)

WE HAVE RECEIVED so many requests for copies of our liturgies that we thought the best thing to do was to publish a St Hilda prayer book. The small group that agreed to try to sort out suitable material for publication found itself going through more than eighty different liturgies, some of them written by our own members, many of them borrowed from other books of prayers. We have tried to select the most usable, though other good material got left on the shelf. We are grateful to those whose prayers have inspired us, and hope others will find them as helpful as we have. Since, as it says in the Preface to the *Alternative Service Book*, 'Christians are formed by the way in which they pray, and the way they choose to pray expresses what they are', we thought we should also say a bit about ourselves, partly to explain our thinking, partly in case it is useful to any group working in the same area.

The St Hilda Community came into existence through the despair and anger of a group of women in the Church of England. At the July meeting of General Synod of 1986, held in York, there was a Measure to allow women priests from other countries – Women Lawfully Ordained Abroad as they were known for the purposes of the Measure – to celebrate Holy Communion in this country. It was a modest proposal, hedged around by strict regulations, but it would have given many Anglicans in this country a chance to experience the ministry of a woman at the altar.

The proposal got a majority in all three houses of Synod, but it did not get the two thirds majority required by Article 8 business; the opposition had been enormously active, threatening schism and all kinds of disaster if the House voted in favour. No, Women Lawfully Ordained Abroad were not wanted by the Church of England, thank you very much.

Eleven years before that vote, in 1975, Synod had decided that there was 'no fundamental objection' to women priests, yet ever afterwards their supporters had watched the issue fudged and delayed on all kinds of pretexts. Many of us felt a deep lack of trust, not simply in the opposition – their stance was plain enough – but in many who claimed to believe in women's orders, but who plainly were in no hurry at all to see women better valued. It was a justice issue, but not only a justice issue; it revealed how deeply anti-woman prejudice was grafted into Anglican theology. For many of us that anti-vote made it clear that the Church was not keeping faith with women. We had submitted to the interminable legal processes and determined delaying tactics with monumental patience. We had listened closely to all the arguments and had fondly imagined we were being listened to in return. Now it became clear that even the most modest of proposals would be defeated, that women were a long way down the Church's list of priorities, that, in the unforgettable phrase of Donald Barnes, they were liable to be 'sacrificed on the altar of ARCIC'. At that point, to use a cheap literary expression, 'something snapped' in many of us. Our trust and patience were exhausted. We believed in the validity of women's orders and wished to see them exercised. On that day, you might say, the St Hilda Community was born.

Following the disgraceful July Synod, in the autumn of 1986, some of us started meeting to design a radical new way of 'being Church'. We did not want to give up our Christian allegiance, still less to found a sect. But we wanted a form of worship – a 'non-sexist liturgy', as we soon began to call it, that gave full space and authority to women, without apology, secrecy, or shame. (Most of us had taken part frequently in eucharists celebrated by women priests in private houses, but since the furore when Liz Canham celebrated at the St Paul's Deanery, and the Bishop of London declared such services 'illegal', we had fallen into the habit of doing so secretly.)

Now we decided that we would hold eucharists openly, to be celebrated by visiting women priests and, not to be underhand, we would advertise them. We wanted men, as well as women, to be an integral part of the Community, because part of what we wanted to learn (and to teach the Church) was a more equal and generous way of gender-relating than any of the churches (even those which already ordained women) seemed to understand. We wanted a Community that worked by consensus and not by hierarchy, because consensus was what, as feminists, we had spent the previous decade carefully exploring. We wanted to call the new group a Community, not because we would be living together but because we wanted to share – gifts, ideas, leadership, vision, and perhaps sometimes possessions and money. We wanted it to embrace anyone who came to it, and our earliest rule was that anyone who came to a liturgy was part of the Community while they were visiting us.

Where could this vibrant body meet? Our first hope was that we might persuade a friendly Vicar to let us meet in his Church, but those whom we approached were nervous, not of us, but of disciplinary action being taken against them. At that moment we learned that Peter Francis, the chaplain of Queen Mary College, in London's East End, was longing to find some way to help the women's movement. He had read an article written by one of us complaining that most clergy did everything, short of actually helping, to make women's ordination a reality, and at that moment resolved to take some action. As a chaplain in a multi-denominational religious set-up he was in a safer position than most parish clergy but, more important, he saw exactly what we were trying to do and why we wanted to do it, and he was prepared to take risks. He offered us the use of the Queen Mary College chapel, St Benet's, for a service every Sunday evening. As it was to turn out, he was actually offering us a great deal more – kindness, ideas, spiritual insight, regular participation, food, tea, coffee, wine, loyalty – in a word, love, though it took us a while to realize the full extent of his concern, and that of his assistant Julie Hare.

*What I like about it, I suppose is that um . . . it's kind of very real – it's more what I imagine the early church would have been like, a small community of people. It's not governed by any kind of hierarchy or predictable order of things, it comes from the heart. . . .*

So, in February 1987, the Community met for the first time in the small, round, domed chapel of St Benet's – there were about eighteen people – and shyly, awkwardly, spelled out what it wanted to do and invited comment. There was an animated discussion. From then on the Community was to meet every Sunday at 6.30 p.m. up until the present day, only missing two Sundays, one of them Christmas Day, and the other the date of an important feminist service in Westminster Abbey.

Within two or three weeks it had selected a name – it had decided to call itself after Hilda of Whitby. She was chosen partly because she was a strong, intelligent woman – according to legend the chairperson of the Synod of Whitby – as someone remarked, a nice change from all those neurotic women saints. She was chosen partly too because she founded, at Whitby, a community of women and men that encouraged the talents of all; they were a lavishly gifted group of scholars and poets, five of the men going on to become bishops. It was only later, when we had listened (on her feast day) to the Venerable Bede's descriptions of Hilda, that another significant thing about her began to appeal to us. Her mother Breguswith, in deep distress at the imprisonment of her husband, Hilda's father, had had a dream that beneath her gown was 'a jewel, who would give light to many'. Unusually for women of her generation, or indeed of subsequent generations, Hilda was born to a mother who passionately believed in her abilities, so that it was scarcely surprising that Hilda had the courage and the confidence to found two monasteries at Hartlepool and Whitby, and to preside for a time over another at Tadcaster. Like Hilda's mother believing in her daughter, we believed in the jewel, not yet fully apparent to the world, of women's spiritual gift.

We advertised our meetings in the *Church Times*, and word of mouth quickly got round the women's networks, so that almost immediately we enjoyed congregations that would put most parish churches to shame. The best advertisement at this stage, however, came from a letter of protest – a sort of Disgusted of Whitby letter – signed by the Vicar, Rural Dean and Bishop of Whitby, together with the Prioress of the Order of the Holy Paraclete, complaining that we were disgracing St Hilda's name, and that the saint would certainly disapprove. We replied politely, pointing out that there was no patent in saints, and that we believed Hilda might have a stomach for what we were doing. As a result we began to receive many sympathetic letters and many more visitors.

The Movement for the Ordination of Women itself had some ambivalent feelings about us. Brought into being by some of its radical members, we were a source of grief and scandal to its more conservative constituency who believed

*I was told by a woman friend about a group that was having a non-sexist liturgy, and I came along and found that not only was it non-sexist but there seemed to be a different atmosphere about the thing altogether. I've been coming for the past three years. It's had its ups and downs because people are only human – they're not perfect – but there's a kind of spark of life and hope about it somehow. . . .*

that MOW's best bet was to have an invariably respectable image, and that St Hilda's growing, and somewhat flamboyant, reputation could only be 'counter-productive'. Yet a number of key members of MOW were loyal supporters.

Slowly, our distinctive liturgies began to take shape in a form that shared leadership between all the participants, that encouraged discussion of what we did, and that emboldened everyone, sooner or later, to design liturgies, with whatever help we could give them. Those who had never written a prayer or shaped a liturgy before were surprised at how much more deeply they had to think about it, what new insights they acquired into the purpose of worship, and the sort of drama that was needed to make it come alive. Some of the nervousness and shyness of 'being in church' dropped away as we entered into a period of experiment. All kinds of symbols were brought to the chapel and shared in interesting ways – grapes, yeast, oil, water, incense. We experimented too with poetry, music and later with dance, a theme explored on page 32 by Lillalou Hughes. Many who thought they hated dancing found that our sort of quiet meditative movement (drawing heavily on circle dancing, of course) filled them with a deep sense of peace and prayer. We liked stillness and silence, but we also did a lot of talking, usually sitting or lying around on the floor, speaking of our beliefs, our distress at the pain of the world or that of the particular friends for whom we prayed, our anger and profound disappointment in the Church. Sometimes the Community consisted mostly of Anglicans, some still working or worshipping within parish churches, but very often there were Catholics, Methodists, Baptists, Quakers, as well as those who had walked out of institutional Christianity, and others who were still seeking for the bare rudiments of faith. Already, our discussions had less of a parochial Anglican flavour – our feet seemed to be set, as it says in the Psalms, in a large room, a larger room than we had begun with. We preceded and followed our meetings with generous cups of tea and coffee, and often ended up drinking wine among the student posters in the St Benet's common-room, unwilling to leave one another. At the least excuse for a feast we brought food to share, though we also

*We had a new woman deacon who was very keen on feminist theology and she dragged me along with her to St Hilda's so she had somebody to go with.*

*So what did you think of it when you got there?*

*I felt the building (St Benet's) was like going into a womb. It had a strong sense of female spirituality and a very strong emphasis on the importance of the feminine . . . it felt rather distant from East London. . . .*

developed habits of going to eat together in the cheap and excellent Indian and Chinese restaurants of the Mile End Road. It was a very happy time – an unforgettable time.

By our first Easter, as Suzanne remembers, the Community had swollen to nearly 100 people, and our reputation had spread widely in the Church. People learned of us in all kinds of ways; one contemplative convent frequently steered a number of visitors in our direction, usually women who were fed up with a sexist Church. We knew, from later snatches of conversation that reached us, that we were discussed extensively among bishops and clergy, not always in complimentary tones. A favourite story was of a priest who called upon the Patriarch of Moscow ready for conversation about Orthodoxy, only to be beset with questions about the St Hilda Community. The Patriarch had read about us in *The Times*. We found too that we were known in Canada, and the USA, in New Zealand and Australia, as visitors made a point of looking us up, and took messages back with them to the other side of the world.

It would be good if we could say that our visitors always had glowing experiences and went home with good stories to tell, but in fact we were, and indeed are, rather 'curate's egg', that is, 'good in parts'. All of us who have been long associated with St Hilda's remember some extraordinary times when Christian fellowship and meanings struck home to us as never before, but there was no guarantee that a casual visitor would find us at our very best. Because of the *ad hoc* nature of our planning, and the fact that there was a good deal of effort involved in our creative liturgies, we also had our bad Sundays, particularly during August when people were away, when there were few people around, and the result could be rather depressing. Unlike church congregations we had no 'leaders' who were supposed to take overall responsibility; decisions were argued through, sometimes very heatedly.

The casual visitor could find her or himself caught in alarming crossfire – we have learned, belatedly, to save our worst rows for a more intimate setting, though again, unlike many churches, we believe anger can be creative and

*I enjoy the discussions and the freedom with which people are able to question or express their doubts and nobody, nobody is looked at as though they are less perfect as a Christian for having doubts; through expressing them people seem to come to a better understanding of what faith's about . . . being in company with people who have had the same experience of feeling oppressed and repressed in the church. Spontaneity. Emphasis not on doing things right or wrong, but on being.*

energy-giving. We should know; we have had quite a lot of it. Sometimes too, visitors were scandalized by finding themselves praying to 'God our Mother', by our accepting attitude to homosexuality or the courage of the Greenham Common women, or by our fierce arguments about the Bible when some Old Testament passage 'got up someone's nose'. Yet others wept to find themselves in the kind of Church they had always dreamed of, one that at least attempted to include anyone and everyone who wished to be included, and where you could scarcely put a foot wrong provided you were genuine. We were, in the main, white and middle-class – it was difficult to see how to correct this without self-conscious exercises which might well have been patronizing – and it took all our energies to provide something worthwhile for the large numbers of people who actually came. We always enjoyed accommodating the odd wanderer from the streets (one of whom I remember asking 'Is this the service for alcoholics?'), patients from the local mental hospital, and casual worshippers who, sometimes to their own surprise, found St Hilda's triggered deep inner pain.

Quite early on we discovered that the supply of 'women lawfully ordained abroad' was intermittent; wishing to have the services of a priest we asked Suzanne Fageol, an American priest studying in England, if she would be 'our' priest, and she took this on rather bravely since it made her life difficult in many parts of the Church where she suddenly became 'tabu' as a preacher and speaker because of her association with us. Greater stresses were to be placed on her than this.

For the first couple of years of the Community we thought and talked a great deal about what to do when no woman priest was forthcoming – when Suzanne was away and no other woman was available. Only once did we ask a male priest to celebrate for us – this was at the leaving party of our beloved Peter Francis. This was not, of course, because we did not appreciate male priests, but rather that St Hilda's, unlike every other church congregation in England, existed to give space to women. Sometimes though, we celebrated as a Community when Suzanne was not there (it was always Suzanne's position that the entire

*A friend of mine saw an advertisement in the Church Times. As a man I had been committed for a long time to women's ordination because I increasingly felt that women had much to offer which was being denied in the life of the church.*

*So when you came what did you feel about it?*

*I found it a tremendously exciting event. It was the first Easter at St Hilda's and it said something that wasn't being said anywhere else in the church. . . .*

Community celebrated, not she herself alone), and in the early days I remember feeling vaguely 'legal' if a male priest was in the congregation and said the eucharistic prayer with us. Later I ceased to feel this. We also invited Methodist, Baptist, and Unitarian ordained women to celebrate for us on occasion, and one of them, the Reverend Ann Arthur, became a very active member of the Community. Among the early regulars were many students and a good sprinkling of men, though women always predominated.

Eighteen months into our existence an extraordinary crisis suddenly struck. Ever since our inception we had attracted an enormous amount of Press interest, and had invitations to write articles, appear on television, and give interviews for newspapers and magazines. In the early days we used to joke about 'moles' from the Alliance for an Apostolic Ministry or Women Against the Ordination of Women lurking in our congregations in order to report us to 'authority', but in the end it was not they, but a journalist from the *Sunday Times*, Charles Oulton, who, presumably looking for a good story, insisted on drawing the Bishop of London's attention to the fact that the Eucharist was being 'irregularly' celebrated at St Benet's. The bishop approached the new chaplain, Peter Francis's successor, who defended us as well as he could, and then politely asked us for an undertaking not to celebrate. Equally politely we refused. Within a few days this had become a *cause célèbre* with the Press eagerly waiting to see what we would do. For the next three weeks we continued to celebrate with an increased congregation, and journalists waiting at the door – many of our friends came to support us, including a yellow labrador.

In the final week a letter reached Suzanne and others in the Community from the solicitors for the London Diocesan Fund. By this time we had learned that although Queen Mary College were sympathetic to us, the chapel was owned by the London Diocese, who thus had the right to threaten us, very dubiously since we were there by invitation and paid a small rent, with a charge for trespass. (We enjoyed joking to one another that whereas Jesus thought trespassers should be forgiven, the Bishop of London preferred the legal

*I'm from an Irish Catholic background and I suppose I value very much the spontaneity and realness and I feel women can come here and be real. And also I like having men with us, and also the feeling that we can include people who may feel they don't belong anywhere. Coming here makes me feel I know who I am. . . .*

*Having lived in England a little over two years, I was looking out for groups, women's groups, where spirituality would be important and I heard about St Hilda's in my wanderings through Quaker groups and other groups, mostly of marginalized women. So I came along a couple of times and now I live a bit nearer I can come more often. . . .*

services of Winckworth and Pemberton.)

Some of us were being hounded by the Press (I remember being rung up at two in the morning), who wanted to know what we proposed to do. Suzanne was virtually under siege – she telephoned once, in some panic, to say that her front garden was full of photographers.

We made our plans by telephone and when we arrived at St Benet's on our final, bitterly cold, night there was a blaze of television lights waiting outside, and reporters from major newspapers. There were also several policemen. 'Why are you here?' I asked one. 'In case there's any trouble,' he replied grimly, 'fighting and that sort of thing', and then, splendidly missing the point, 'But don't you worry, dear. We'll protect you.' (When the service was over I went back into St Benet's for the last time and made him a cup of tea. 'I don't get it,' he said, referring to the service. 'You all seem harmless enough to me.')

Suzanne celebrated that night in the car park, flanked by two women deacons who cared enough to put their jobs on the line, and surrounded by a congregation of about a hundred. The next week, forced out of St Benet's, we celebrated two hundred yards down the road in the Bow Road Church (a church with both Anglican and Methodist congregations) which had welcomed us with open arms, and which has been unfailingly hospitable to us ever since.

The talk and excitement went on for weeks, with Suzanne distinguishing herself on television, and the Community receiving every sort of media coverage. One quiz show even had the question 'Who celebrated Communion in a car park this week and why?' Sudden fame brought many new members to St Hilda's and as we settled into our new quarters we were in good heart.

In February 1989 Barbara Harris was consecrated bishop in Boston, and a few of us flew over to share the celebrations, while those left behind held a special liturgy for Barbara. Conversations with some American women – the Episcopal Women's Caucus – suggested that they might be willing to help with funds for St Hilda's and slowly we worked out more ambitious plans – to host some conferences, to publish a book, to pay for some regular co-ordinating

*St Hilda's has been very good for me because as a deacon I normally can't enjoy my own worship very well. I have to lead it, I have to be responsible for it, and although sometimes I'm responsible for a service here it feels different, and most of the time I can just worship as one of the Community. . . .*

**13**

work. It also started the thought of paying Suzanne on a part-time basis – the rest of the time she would follow her vocation elsewhere.

Unexpectedly, the decision about this was one which shook the Community to its roots. Suzanne was loved and admired by everyone, but she herself had fears that using her as a 'proper priest' would 'dis-enable' the Community and encourage us to leave everything to her. Others in the Community felt that, while still wanting to be supportive of the movement for women priests, we would do better to see ourselves as a lay movement, with lay people exercising all functions. Others again felt commitment to the political statement about women priests originally made when St Hilda first started. All of these discussions showed how deeply the St Hilda experience had opened us to an understanding of many important issues besides gender – in particular the issue of the relationship of priest and laity, but also the question of how far we wanted to be 'just' an Anglican community when we had such a strong experience of ecumenism. So devastating was the disagreement that followed, despite brave efforts at reconciliation on all sides, that we had to ask an outside facilitator, Jeanette Renouf, to spend a day sorting us out.

As a result of that discussion, Suzanne became committed to St Hilda on a regular basis, yet it was as if the Community could not get over its struggle. Numbers fell away, a kind of gloom enveloped us, and for some months we questioned openly whether our days of usefulness were over and we would do better to close down. People stopped volunteering for jobs or to write liturgies, and some of our most faithful members seemed to lose heart. Not that life was entirely lacking – a new St Hilda group sprang up that began to meet monthly in West London. (Several other groups in various parts of the country had imitated our original experiment under different names.) But Suzanne at length said she felt in a false position in the Community and, to our deep regret, felt she could not be 'our' priest, though she would remain part of the Community.

In the following few weeks there were intensive questionings about what we should do, and then a dozen or so of us met together and found ourselves drafting

> *What I like best is all the ups and downs, and the fact that it's my only church and a place where one can explore where one is spiritually, be nourished by what one hears. I think what I enjoy most of all is the discussion following the readings as not being a theologian I find that quite exciting and I really love the differences that people pick up in any one passage. I also like to feel that one can worship and at the same time be joyful, angry, questioning and all that I find here. . . .*

*I came because one of the Sisters came. I had been going to an established church for a long time and I felt that it no longer met my needs. I was tired of having a hierarchy where one person was more powerful than another, and I didn't feel that my needs as a single woman were met at all. What I like about St Hilda's is that there is no leader although I think sometimes it feels a bit directionless. I like very much the variety – the candles, the meditation, the circle dancing. . . .*

*After the Pentecost celebration I started because although I was very happy in the local church in which I was involved – it is about 95% black and also an exciting congregation to be part of, nevertheless this was another place which affirmed something which was important to me. . . .*

new plans for a stronger St Hilda's. The organization, so often a source of quarrelling between us – 'I did all the work last week, in fact I'm always doing it' – now became the target for thoughtful reform, with a co-ordinator, Pat Willmitt, helping things to run smoothly. Suddenly we began to remember how enormously we had enjoyed St Hilda's in the past, and new ideas began to flood in, the most important of which is the value of the laity. But the secret of making an enterprise like St Hilda's work is imagination, hard work, love, and the difficult spirit of forgiveness, which alone produce the sort of bonding which makes a community rich and rewarding. I guess four years have taught us that much – as well as a readiness to be endlessly open to new members and new ideas. We feel like survivors, which we are.

It has been such an overwhelming experience in itself that we have not often stopped to look at ourselves in a wider context of historical antecedents and reforming significance. I suppose that we inherit something from contemporary liberation theology, from the 'base communities' of South America and other parts of the world who have felt that the Christian life that teemed within them was perceived as a threat by the traditional churches, and that they could not be fully themselves amid such deadness and lack of imagination. The women and men of St Hilda's needed to work out a pattern, as yet unimaginable in many, perhaps all, of the institutional churches of this country, of a community where women were not patronized and ignored, and where it was safe to be fully themselves. Yet I believe that it is not enough for a group like St Hilda's simply to 'go off', necessary as that may be as a temporary expedient, but we must rather seek to maintain a dialogue so that both traditionalists and reformers struggle with the reality of the others' existence. For traditionalists are always in danger of life-denying rigidity, and reformers are always in danger of eccentricity and 'remnant psychology', the paranoia of being an outsider.

Such dialogues are slow and difficult, but we hope that our existence has made it harder for the churches to condescend to women, and for women to collude with that process. Then we shall not have struggled in vain.

## Celebrating Experience

**Suzanne Fageol**

Once upon a time, a group of people who called themselves 'the Christians' lived on the plains of certainty. Those who lived beyond their borders were referred to as 'the non-Christians'. Since they had never gone beyond the plains of certainty, . . . the people knew what was wrong and right, what they should and should not do and believe. They did not need to know themselves because they existed in the mirror of the other. What is yet to be, they said, is ordained in the past . . . everyone had their place, both men and girls. There was no need for change. . . .

One day a spirit of experience blew in the land. A few felt the cold gust blow across the sunlit way. . . . Many of the plains people ignored experience and . . . built strong walls to protect themselves from the spirit. . . . Some of them believed that the wind came from enemies beyond the way. They shouted in the name of the way that the breezes cease. . . .

Beth Hamilton, *The Journey*[1]

WOMEN'S THEOLOGICAL experiments with their spiritual experience have blown a new wind into the church. The church, which resides on the plain of certainty, has, in turn, shouted for the breezes to cease. But the Spirit has called us and we cannot be stopped from journeying into a new land. This new territory is elusive – familiar and unknown, dark and light, formed and unformed, beautiful and dreadful. There are mountains to climb and valleys to traverse. The forests seem chaotic and the lakes unfathomable. Mists and maelstroms appear everywhere. Some wanderers turn back to safety. Others meander off the way altogether in pain. In the middle of such a journey, in the midst of the whirlwinds in which we find ourselves, where can we find a haven for rest, reflection and relaxation? Where can we find faithful companions, women and men, with whom we can share our travel stories and the visions of our destination? Where can we find support for and celebration of the journey itself?

The creation of the St Hilda Community is one answer to these questions. It was founded primarily as a worship community where women and men together could experience the full ministry of women and the freedom to express and receive the broader wisdom of our Christian heritage and women's spiritual offerings in language which excludes no person and no image of God. What does this look like on a practical level?

When St Hilda's first came together, in February 1987, our first step was community-building. Although we knew right from the group's conception that we wanted to provide a public, advertised place to experience the full ministry of women priests, being feminist meant it was important to us to establish intimacy and relationship with each other. By coming together initially in non-eucharistic worship, we could develop friendship. We would have opportunities to get to know one another as human beings through dialogue about our common purpose and through sharing our views on faith and God. As different members took responsibility for providing liturgical material for worship, we established a pattern of equality between women and men, clergy and laity. Everyone was included and encouraged to exercise whatever gifts of ministry they brought. Community decisions, administrative and liturgical, were made by consensus. Anyone who was present on a given evening was a member of the community and therefore had the right to speak and be included in any decision-making process. We also chose Easter as the date when we would hold the first openly advertised eucharist with a woman celebrant.

Since I was resident in England pursuing my doctoral studies, I was asked if I would be willing to act as the community's priest. This invitation was issued on the understanding that my ministry would be public and that I would step aside from presiding at the eucharist to allow other women priests visiting the country to be invited to celebrate during their time here. That Easter Sunday, in 1987, saw St Benet's chaplaincy at Queen Mary College filled to overflowing with people who came to join us in celebrating the Feast of the Resurrection.

Due to problems already mentioned, created by the Bishop of London, we were forced to use the chaplaincy common room, adjacent to the chapel, for our

Are there things you don't like about St Hilda's?

*No, I don't think so. It's just like any other group, ups and downs.*

*I feel sometimes there's quite a strong feeling of conflict. But I like very much the company of women and feeling that we are all much more equal.*

Easter celebration. This location and set of circumstances actually enhanced the atmosphere. It allowed us to make creative use of the space. The chapel at St Benet's is round, rather womb-like (or in this case, tomb-like). We removed the altar and the lector's stand (there are no pews or chairs) and left an empty chapel with a single candle burning in the middle as a reminder of Christ's empty tomb. We placed the altar just on the threshold of the entrance to the chapel, so I could celebrate with my back to the chapel, but just on the edge. My heels were one inch from the carpet boundary which divided the two spaces. Everyone, therefore, had the view of a woman priest on the verge of the 'inner sanctum' but excluded from it, and the view of the lighted candle in the empty chapel.

We began with a dance – to consecrate the worship space. We sang of Mary Magdalene, first to see the risen Christ. We called God 'Mother', the God of Sarah, Our Creator, Redeemer, Sustainer; and we called ourselves, female and male, sacred and equal in the image of God. We anointed each other with the oil of forgiveness. We celebrated the paschal mystery together. We passed around the freshly baked bread and the wine, communicating each other. We proclaimed that we, too, had risen; that we would never again return to being spiritually and liturgically dead. Finally, we blessed each other. Many male priests joined us in addition to women deacons (then deaconesses), religious and lay people. There were: authors, artists, two deans of cathedrals, householders, students, a security guard, doctors, lawyers, a road sweeper, parents, children, secretaries and an economist; a broad spectrum of humanity. The most surprising and welcoming thing to some of us was the number of non-Anglicans who joined us. There were Roman Catholics, Quakers, Unitarians, Methodists and Baptists; people from many denominations and none. There were also present a Buddhist, a Jew and a Muslim. After the service, we all stayed on for a party. No one could quite believe that we had managed to celebrate publicly a vision of the future church so openly, so joyfully and with such a sense of freedom. We were absolutely ebullient. The symbolism of

*I do think we need to be better at our communication and organization.*

*I sometimes don't like the fact that because it's so unorganized it falls to the more regular attenders to do more . . . it gets taken for granted. Sometimes too I think there's a sort of pressure that comes in with some who are still very heavily involved in their ordinary church, to do things the way they've always been done traditionally. And we get stuck in the middle between the old and the new working out, so sometimes there is this pull to go backwards. . . .*

women being almost, but not fully, equal in the church together with the symbolism of the light of our resurrection and victory of life over spiritual death was powerful that evening. It remains with many people even now.

Encapsulated in that one evening is the essence of everything for which the St Hilda Community stands, theologically and liturgically. From it emerged all the issues and practices which were to anchor us and keep us dialoguing about our diversity. This essence falls into two broad areas – ecclesiology and liturgy. With regard to the former, our concept of church and ministry, there is a spectrum. The overall concept which contains this spectrum states that 'church' is the gathered body of Christ. It includes those who are physically present for worship and those who are gathered in spirit. 'Ministry' is that in which we all engage in one form or another, according to each person's sense of their vocation. Ministry is multifaceted; therefore, that area to which one person feels called one week may change the next week. Primary, however, is the fact that each person actively engages in some form of ministry each time they are present. This ministry could range from facilitating the overall pattern of worship, to dancing, to participating in the intercessions, to creative listening. There is also less distinction made between the functions of those who are ordained and those who are lay. Lay people preside at the 'eucharist' and ordained people make tea! Because of our denominational diversity, when ordained women from any church exercise their sacramental ministry, little emphasis is placed on the source of their authority.

There is great interest and much debate, too, about the true nature of priesthood, and indeed, about the function and role of all ordained ministry. This creative tension has been the focus of liturgies themselves. Women deacons and laity struggle with what is appropriate for them to do sacramentally. The community struggles with whether a deacon's mass is appropriate when celebrated by a woman deacon using elements previously consecrated by male priests and whether a lay-led celebration is eucharist or agape. These kinds of ongoing tensions help us all think through our doctrine of church and

> *I don't like the bickering, and the arguments after some of the services. Angry energy can ruin the service. There's nowhere for it to go afterwards, so we row. I don't like the fact that we don't seem to be drawing closer as a community, we seem to have got so far and then remained like separate beads on a necklace, not integrated. We don't seem to have a common purpose any longer – like we did in the early days when we were very directly challenging the church and they were questioning our existence. I'm not sure our internal life is growing. . . .*

sacrament. In this sense, conflict becomes creative. It brings clarity, tolerance of diversity and deeper engagement with one another.

Liturgically speaking, the scope of possibilities is limitless. Certain elements have become more or less permanent fixtures. With some features drawn from liturgy composed for the Women in Theology liturgy group, they include: spatial arangement in the form of a circle, group reflection on readings, mutual absolution, free intercession and mutual blessing. Our usual practice incorporates a reading of some kind during worship. Often the readings are those appointed for that particular Sunday in the lectionary of the Church of England. Sometimes alternative scripture passages or pieces of prose or poetry are chosen because of their relevance to the liturgical theme. The seasons of the church calendar are observed. Our matronal feast day is marked, in part, by a reading about Hilda of Whitby's life and ministry. Following the reading, there is silence, then a group reflection on the reading lasting about twenty minutes.

Mutual absolution takes the form of a shared general confession, drawn from various sources, feminist and other. After this comes individual absolution where each person, in turn, faces their neighbour, makes the sign of the cross on the forehead (or holds the other's hands), sometimes anointing the person with scented oil, and says, 'God forgives you, forgive others, forgive yourself', or similar words. The practice continues around the circle until everyone has received absolution. This sacramental act, normally preserved as the priest's, is powerful when done personally and as a shared ministry of the whole body of Christ. The depth of forgiveness, given and received, brings us all closer to God and to each other as images of God incarnate.

Intercessions, too, take on a quality of intimacy seldom experienced in formal church settings. There is always a bowl of sand, symbolic of the desert wilderness, set in the centre of the circle with a single lighted candle in its centre. Next to the bowl sits a basket of small votive candles. During the intercessions, people are free to light a candle from the basket and place it in the sand while naming, either silently or aloud, their petition or thanksgiving.

*Sometimes it gets to feel a bit tentative and fragile, though maybe that's saying something about me too. I wonder sometimes when the numbers get fewer if it's going to go on. . . .*

Sometimes flowers are substituted for candles, and an empty vase is placed beside the bowl. The end of this section of the liturgy yields a bowl of light or a vase overflowing with flowers, reminding us of our collective humanity and of the light and beauty of God's response to us.

Beyond these semi-permanent features in our liturgy, anything goes. A glance at the liturgy section of this book gives some idea of the creativity of the members of St Hilda's. The liturgies have been drawn from feminist sources. Some are from one published source entirely; some are compilations from various sources and others are original material from group members. Each has created a space for experimentation. Each has put us in touch with our deeper feelings and our spirituality.

Sometimes, liturgies have provoked deep anger. Often they have brought up hidden issues between women and men or conflict regarding the use of scripture. I think particularly of a service taken from Rosemary Ruether's *Women-church*. It was an exorcism of scripture passages detrimental to women. After hearing read aloud all the bible passages which denigrate women, the anger and depression felt by the women present was so strong that one woman found it extremely difficult to receive or give absolution to the men seated on either side of her. We stopped the liturgy for a discussion and venting of our feelings. While the conflict was not immediately resolved, the space and time to give care to one another (rather than worrying about finishing on time or at all) was welcomed and appreciated. Nurturing and care-giving always take precedence over worship. If we cannot care for one another, how can we possibly hope to incarnate effectively the One in whose name we gather to worship?

Another example of liturgy which allowed great depth of feeling to emerge was of an entirely different nature. It was a Palm Sunday liturgy composed by a group member. Simple in form, it spoke and enacted the passion of Holy Week in a participatory way which spiritually immersed us in the events of Jesus' last days as if we ourselves had been present. Several branches of budding and just-blossoming forsythia were laid in the centre of the circle. In silence they were

*It's quite difficult to keep in contact with people as you just come here on a Sunday and then go away again so the worship is quite valuable but it's difficult to build deeper relationships with people. . . .*

*As a Methodist lay preacher I have sometimes looked on with bewilderment at the vehemence and anger the issue of women's ordination rouses among Anglicans. Sometimes it has spilled over into the Community as those hurt by institutional religion have turned and hurt one another. . . . God is part of all our messy experience.*

passed around with the instruction that each of us was to strip a bit from the branch. The denuded branches, empty of new growth and flowers, were placed back in the centre of the circle for contemplation. As we each realized our potential for destroying the Tree of Life, we were humbled by our failure to receive Christ and by our power to tear the Christ energy from other human beings. Many women also connected this symbolic act with the ways in which they, as images of God incarnate, had been violated.

The passion of St Hilda's liturgies speaks, too, of joy. One gift of feminist theology to the church is its insistence that worship and spirituality must be embodied. We have our relationships with God and with others as flesh and blood creatures. For too long, however, the emphasis in patriarchal theology has been on affirming the spirit and denying and denigrating the flesh. In this context, women have accepted, both for themselves and for western culture and society, all that men see as sinful and dangerous about the body. Any references to bodily functions and sexuality have equated women with evil – for instance, when women dare to envisage Christ in the sculpted form of a female Christa on the cross as in the sculpture by Edwina Sandys. Men have blamed us for perpetrating the spiritual crime of humanizing God. The St Hilda Community is one example of women's challenge to reclaim the human body, especially the feminine one, as a celebration of our creation in God's image and of ourselves as divine reflections of the human nature of God.

This reclamation of our wholeness is manifested at St Hilda's in many ways. It is reflected in our attention to the worship space itself. The circle is a symbol of containment – the womb, the vessel – which includes and births the divine in us. Dance provides another mode of incorporating our spirituality. Dance allows us to express bodily the joy and pain of our lives, the giving and receiving of the sacredness of life. We dance to celebrate our divinity and our humanity, to consecrate ourselves and our worship to the glory of God, to centre and still ourselves in meditation, to symbolize our solidarity with the oppressed of the world, and to announce and solidify our relationship to one another as the body

*Like any community it had its ups and downs – there was something very realistic about the way it dealt with them. But everyone was accepted – there was a lot of new life in the kind of liturgies being produced, both in terms of variations on the traditional themes of the eucharist, but also new ways of treating life as something that was whole and not something set apart. An immense sense of wholeness.*

of Christ. We dance, like Christ, as holy fools, to heal the brokenness of the world, incarnate in our broken selves.

If we are to embody our spirituality and our theology, it must be reflected in our language, both about ourselves and God. One bridge between our bodies and our language is our feelings. Such feelings as vulnerability, weakness and helplessness have traditionally been interpreted by our culture as belonging to the psychological character of women, and labelled negative. Feminism tends to view them as constructive and positive essential human feelings. Women have discovered that vulnerability, weakness and helplessness are both sources of strength and the basis for a more advanced form of living. As we allow ourselves to admit that these feelings are real and allow ourselves to feel them in our bodies, they become sources of inspiration and avenues for deeper relationship with God and with each other. To admit fear openly, and to identify needs accurately, makes turning to others and to God and asking for help easier. This process further demands emotional connectedness with another being. It facilitates a language of engagement arising from our bodies.

It is the language of engagement which is used between women and God in scripture. Remember the woman who touched Jesus' cloak? It is also the mode of language in which women engage when identifying God. Janet Morley, a feminist liturgical author and a member of St Hilda's, writes for us in this way when she uses such phrases as: 'vulnerable God', 'so we may show forth his brokenness', 'for on this night you were delivered as one of us . . . needy and naked', 'you emptied yourself of power', and 'inspire our weakness'.[2]

Beyond the language of engagement, we have also felt the need for language which includes images that broaden and deepen our understanding of the mystery of God in non-patriarchal terms. As feminists, we look to the sources of creation. These sources of feminine creation, contained in goddess and Celtic spiritual traditions, help satisfy our quest for new images. In addition, many are compatible with Christianity. They speak of the wider connections between humanity and the rest of creation. They connect us, on a global level, with the

Were there things you didn't like?

*There were times when the professional in me (if you will forgive the expression) felt, 'Oh dear, if only things could run more smoothly.'*

Do you mean liturgically?

*Yes. Yet when things did not go smoothly I liked the way it was accepted, it wasn't, 'Oh help, we got that wrong.'*

elemental sources of life itself – air, water, food and shelter – and with Mother Earth. Prayers to the earth, as the matrix for the source of life, and to the elements, characterize our interdependence with the created order and with God our Creator.

Theologically speaking, this is the doctrine of panentheism, i.e., God is in everything and everything is in God. This source of relationality is also found within the Christian tradition, although historically it has been relegated to the sidelines of orthodoxy by those in ecclesiastical power. To speak too much of nature and natural processes, like birth and creation, has been deemed by the patriarchy as pagan. Analogies drawn between the creative functions of women and nature are dangerous; perhaps because men then feel excluded from creative possibilities and power. St Hilda's liturgies consciously work at redeeming these traditions for the church. We draw on sources from the Hebrew bible, the psalms, and the medieval Christian mystics, as well as from goddess and Celtic material.

As Christian women we need to celebrate our creativity, on all levels. We are called to open the church, and men, as well as ourselves, to the idea that we are originally blessed as created in the image of God and as connected to the rest of creation. We want to demonstrate every human being's potential for creation and creativity. We want to proclaim our right to such creativity as good, natural and holy. St Hilda's members have constructed whole liturgies around the celebration of God as our Mother, as the one who gives birth to and nurtures us into creative adulthood. The Hebrew bible is a rich source for such wisdom and celebration. There we find images of God as Holy Wisdom who teaches us spiritual discernment and God as 'ruach', the feminine wind-energy who brings creation out of chaos. These are but a few of the themes we have explored in worship.

As a continuation of this process we celebrate the wise women of scripture and tradition who have revealed God and hidden parts of ourselves to us. Both in their strengths and in their weaknesses, they have shown us ways of empower-

There were always fewer men than women in the Community. I wondered how that felt to you as a man?

*In a very gentle way it brought home to me the sense of there being a difference, yet not a difference. It came over most in business matters – in most business meetings I have been to there have been a predominance of men yet at St Hilda's business meetings I was sometimes the only man present. Women did things differently.*

How?

*I think there was always a sense of looking for a consensus. Sometimes, of course, it did come to a case of saying well, who's in favour and who is against. But always there was a desire to get to something that was generally accepted, to carry people with us, and that was quite refreshing. There was something too about the interconnectedness of things – peace, justice, a sense of creation.*

ment and images of connectedness. They give us alternative ways of ministering to each other and relating to God. Sarah had the courage to venture into the unknown, leaving everything behind. Deborah used her gift of wisdom as a judge. Mary, the mother of Jesus, showed endurance under oppression. Mary Magdalene had courage to fulfil her ministry in the face of opposition. Hildegard of Bingen and Teresa of Avilá reconnected themselves with creativity. Julian of Norwich taught people to name their experience of Christ as their Mother. All of them allow us to proclaim ourselves as lovers and friends of God.

Inevitably, there are shifts in emphasis as the St Hilda Community grows and changes. New issues for exploration emerge as older issues continue to engage us. Definitions of community, ministry and liturgy remain elusive. But fluidity is a mark of feminist theology. As women's experiences change and grow, so too do our ideas about ourselves and God. For those people who honour tradition and stability, this can be exasperating. For those who wish to continue the spiritual journey with short rests in a refreshing oasis, this is exciting. The St Hilda Community is both oasis and journey for many Christians. We still give hospitality to women ordained abroad. We still wrestle with the issues of priesthood and mutual ministry. We struggle with our community identity. We witness to the world our prophetic vision. We do all these things and more from a feminist perspective in the hope that those who have ears to hear and eyes to see will understand and join our dream of creating a new kind of church. It is a church whose central focus is the people, the body of Christ. It is a church where equality in the sight of God is given to all women and men because they are the image of the divine in human form. It is a church which nurtures, nourishes and encourages each person to find and speak about the God in their hearts. It is a church which understands that interdependence and an ethic of care are the primary ingredients of a worship community. For only as we respect one another in worship and in language can we see ourselves as builders of a new creation. The kingdom/queendom of God is among us – and is us. We are co-creators with God of our lives and of our world. 'May the God who dances in

**Do you think that was peculiar to this Community or is more to do with attitudes held by women generally?**

*It is hard to answer because many women like the traditional hierarchical structures – it felt more like the experience one has in a black community of struggling against something and struggling for something. But although there was a sense of struggle, it was accompanied by a sense of celebration, and the feeling that struggling is not just a case of pain and hardship and oppression but that there's something you can affirm there as well.*

**There's a real excitement in it?**

*That's right, that's right.*

creation, who embraces us with human love, who shakes our lives like thunder, bless us and drive us out with power to fill the world with her justice, Amen.'[3]

I first came to St Hilda's as a theological student. We used to come all the way down from Oxford, and it was absolute bliss after the rather austere prayer at college; it was just wonderful to be able to come into more relaxed surroundings. Although I don't come very often it is very good to know that St Hilda's is here. Some kind of vision for something new and different in the Church, which is something to do with being open and flexible. That we are able to allow each individual to contribute in some way – that's very important to me. Because we're such a very widespread, scattered Community it's sometimes hard to know how it does all happen.

NOTES

[1]Beth Hamilton, 'The Journey', in Rosemary Radford Ruether, *Womanguides: Readings Toward a Feminist Theology* (Boston: Beacon Press, 1985), excerpts from pp.251–2.
[2]Janet Morley, *All Desires Known* (London: Women in Theology and Movement for the Ordination of Women, 1988), p.38 and p.48.
[3]ibid., p.48.

## The Nitty-Gritty:
## Organisation
## and Practicalities
### *Pat Willmitt*

From the first heady days of the St Hilda Community at St Benet's four main stages can be distinguished in our organisational and structural evolution before we got to where we now are. The transitions were not always easy and we usually didn't realise at the time that we were undergoing a process of necessary change but tended to feel rather glum about our prospects, sometimes wondering whether we wanted to go on.

Stage 1

These were the exhilarating days when a broad spectrum of exuberant worshippers turned up. Liberation euphoria was in the air and we felt we had every reason to be celebrating. This was the time when I first became involved in what the St Hilda Community stood for.

In those days there was very little in the way of practicalities to be attended to and hardly any organisation was necessary. Our self-consciousness at that time was simply as a worship group. As long as we had non-hierarchical participation, inclusive language and women celebrants it felt OK and there was never a shortage of people putting their names down on the rota to take a turn at producing a liturgy. All the rest of us had to do was turn up for the worship – and for the parties. Every three weeks or so there seemed to be some sort of party afterwards in the arm-chaired comfort and intimacy of the Students' Union common room adjoining St Benet's chapel. It was either somebody's birthday, somebody was leaving London or had just arrived in London, it was Easter, Pentecost, Advent or St Hilda's birthday or we just felt it would be good to have a get-together afterwards.

At St Benet's all the practicalities were taken care of for us. Coffee, etc. and everything needed for refreshments was laid on. The chapel was circular and the position of the altar and seating arrangements were ideal for us so no shifting of furniture needed to be done before we could start. There was not even a problem about the key and how we would get in as a number of chaplaincy workers and students who worshipped with us lived in flats above the chaplaincy. We often did not bother to put out an offertory plate as there was nothing we needed to buy, though we soon corrected this, partly to pay the modest rent, and partly, on occasion, to give to women's charities.

So, as far as practicalities and organisation went it was easy for us at St Benet's, leaving us free to laugh, sing and dance and we certainly did that. And I think that through the fun we had together we became stronger and more confident, the women particularly. I remember how, at Advent, a woman made a 'Freudian' slip reading the lesson and read out clearly and definitely, 'Now Joseph being just a man. . . .' This caused great hilarity, coming as an especially welcome relief to those of us who'd sat through morning sermons hearing how much more difficult the Nativity had been for poor Joseph than for Mary.

STAGE 2

How deep did it all go? That seemed to become one of the questions when we found ourselves at Bow Road Church, having been thrown out of St Benet's. We were extremely grateful to Bow Road Church for their immediate offer of premises, and their kindness to us since has been unfailing, but the very different situation meant that we had to start to give serious consideration to practical issues and become more organised. From the intimacy of St Benet's we had been forced to move to a rather large, bare hall and some of us found the ambience inhibiting and grieved for St Benet's. The drama of our eviction meant that the 'real' world had come home to us with something of a jolt, in more ways than one. We had to provide our own wine and bread, as well as tea/coffee/milk; had to arrange for somebody to be there every week early with the key; had to ensure that somebody replied to the many letters we began to get after the famous car-park Eucharist; each week before worship started the small altar had to be brought out, the lectern moved back, the seating arrangements changed and all had to be put back afterwards; somebody had to sort and mark the dozens of copies of dozens of liturgies which we had by this time collected. In our new Methodist-based home we rather missed the wine drinking we'd enjoyed at our St Benet's parties.

We felt welcomed and supported by our hosts, and the basics were usually done. We met every Sunday without a break and people were always able to get in. In that time we produced three newsletters to over 200 people who had signed our address book and asked for a newsletter. Any new person coming at this time would probably not have been aware of any stress. It was only those who'd known the exhilarating days of St Benet's who noticed the difference and sensed the strains developing.

For me, it was a *déjà vu* experience to have landed at Bow Road Methodist Church again. Fourteen years previously I'd departed from the Church of England in pain and disgust over their official attitude and my local rector's attitude to divorced women. By some fluke of circumstances then I'd landed at Bow Road Methodist Church which had a very radical minister, brought my son to Sunday school there and been a regular worshipper for four years before I moved up North for ten years. Returning to London, I'd been giving the Church of England a 'second chance' for two years but, just prior to hearing about St Hilda had decided that membership of any formal, official church was probably not right for me. So it was strange to feel I'd landed at BRMC for the second time in my life and due to similar reasons as the first time – reasons to do with the Church of England's prejudice.

## STAGE 3

This is the stage where the regular 'core' members of the St Hilda Community consciously tried to get organised in order to cope responsibly with everything and by and large it worked.

There had been a resistance to structure and organisation and for good reasons. We feared we'd lose our characteristic openness to change and our

I came because I heard Suzanne give a talk. I was struck at once by the level of participation. As a Roman Catholic I cannot participate in any shape or guise in my Church. Even if I have a very sensitive parish priest other than reading and giving out communion I am invisible. So this is a very enabling experience – you do certain things very carefully and you don't have to ask people for permission. Women are very often traumatized. The problem, of course, with every organization that is a non-bureaucratic one, is how do you carry on without an institution. It may be that if the personal charisma goes out then the whole thing falls down. But if it does fall down then that may be a sign of the Spirit. If you keep it going artificially with a very efficient and well-oiled machine of bureaucracy, then you may be answering to a need that is not there. So I don't mind if something collapses, because it had its place, and if it was important it will come back, perhaps in a different guise.

flexibility and that we'd then gradually slide into being just like the institutionalised churches, which we saw as bureaucratic and fearful of change. There seemed to be an unspoken consensus that we'd do better just to muddle our way through rather than risk ending up with a PCC! From there, we feared, it would be a short step to starting to worry about the deathwatch beetle!

It was specific external circumstances that motivated and impelled us to become more organised. Basically, it had to do with two factors. One was the offer of money from the USA Women's Caucus of the Episcopal Church for the furtherance of the St Hilda Community's work and the other was the fact that we wanted to employ Suzanne Fageol as our priest if we could find a way to do so.

During this period we finally got a bank account opened in the name of the St Hilda Community, and we started a weekly log book. In this we entered the name of the person responsible for worship, the number who attended, the amount of the offertory, any expenses reimbursed, and anything out of the way that occured.

For a while we experimented with sub-groups, handling finance, communications, advertising, special events and liturgy, but they never really got off the ground, partly because so many of us were so enormously busy. We were better at throwing in a lot of energy for one particular event than regular committee work.


STAGE 4

This basically can be described as the stage, which lasted for several months, during which it all somehow seemed to be left to the same two or three people to do everything with pressures building up from all directions. Some of the drama of St Hilda seemed to have evaporated, and with it some of our enthusiasm. Many of the regular attenders had either moved from London, were ill, or were going through busy or difficult times; we were having some difficulty finding people to sign up on the rota to be responsible for worship although there had been a steady trickle, week by week, of new people unable to feel at home in their local church.

An emergency meeting was called of regular and committed members at which meeting people cleared the air with their grievances and we had a good discussion about where we were and where we wanted to be. It was considered that we'd moved on a long way in consciousness from being simply a worship group and now saw that there was a lot more for us to be doing. We wanted to develop our range of activities, increase our membership, spend the money from the USA wisely, support and empower the people who came to the St Hilda Community looking for succour, encourage and support secular womens' self-help groups, challenge the prejudice and ignorance of the official church, and last but not least we wanted to cease exploiting and taking advantage of the goodwill of the handful of supporters. We accepted that it was necessary but not sufficient to be so well-intentioned, and that we'd have to grasp the nettle, as it were, and risk taking on responsibility for moderate structure and organisation.

*What I like is passing round the bread and wine from one to another, and I like saying your own intercession.*

CONCLUSION

If the moving out from St Benet's into the wilderness was a test then I think we've passed it. Although it's not been easy we have shown ourselves capable of sticking together through sombre times. The trick is to find ways of combining a celebratory and liberated attitude to life with a responsible amount of organisation – just enough and no more – to find beauty and joy in our quest for truth and justice. At least, that's the vision I'm seeking to share.

## Finding Our Balance: Dance at St Hilda's
*Lillalou Hughes*

I FIRST CAME ACROSS circle dancing at the Bristol Cancer Help Centre. It was a revelation to me. Suddenly I felt properly joined to the earth after years, it seemed, of being caught in a spiritual limbo between heaven and earth. The contact with the floor, or with the ground out of doors, roots us in unity, harmony and healing.

I had always felt awkward about dancing, as if I had been born with two left feet, and it was wonderful to feel held in the circle by the joined hands, and to find my balance; above all to realize that if I just kept moving the world did not come to an end if I got the steps wrong. The dancing filled me with energy and relaxed me; a sense of well-being overcame me. As my confidence grew I became more deeply aware of the group with whom I danced; a oneness developed as the rhythm took hold of me. And it was fun!

I found a group in London to dance with and gradually discovered about circle dancing, or sacred dancing as some prefer to call it. It was introduced to Britain at Findhorn in the early seventies by Bernhard Wosein, a German ballet master. The dances are drawn from the great wealth of ancient dances of Greece, the Slavic countries, the Jewish and Celtic traditions. These have inspired new compositions and choreography and there are now many new circle dances, sometimes using folk songs and contemporary tunes.

When St Hilda's included circle dancing in its liturgies, I introduced dances there and gradually confidence as a teacher grew. So often liturgies are wordy things, with faith expressed in a very cerebral fashion. It is so good to use our bodies, to bring our whole person to God, and to deepen the mood of a liturgy. There are dances which fit every part of the liturgy – greetings dances, meditative dances, dances based on biblical texts, dances for the Peace, dances for festivals. Many of them are simple enough for anyone to do which makes for a good start; before long we can take risks and learn more complicated dances with more intricate steps and sophisticated rhythms.

Circle-dance tapes with instruction booklets can be obtained, and many

*I heard about St Hilda through my mother and my reasons for coming were just disillusionment with the established church. Being unable to sit through a church service any more because I can't help making the same sort of analysis of the language, the analysis of what's going on that I apply in my everyday work of education. If I was hearing children in school having to sit through that I'd make a horrendous report. I feel I can't listen to it myself, and that any help I could give wouldn't be accepted at this stage. . . . This place is lovely when I get the chance to come. The joy of this is that the language doesn't get in the way, that everyone is welcoming, is accepting, that I have to join in, which is important to me – the first time when I joined in the eucharistic prayer was an incredible experience. The most moving thing was to say what the male priest had said.*

circle-dance groups advertise in local libraries. A local teacher may be willing to arrange a teaching afternoon or evening for you. Tapes are available from Dancing Circles, PO Box 26, Glastonbury, Somerset BA6 9YA.

# Part Two

## Introducing a Service

At St Hilda all our services take place in a circle, so that everyone can see everyone else, and there are no 'special' places. Before we sit down, however, we try to welcome people as they arrive, though sometimes shyness or carelessness spoils the intention. It is an ongoing effort to remember to talk to and welcome people we don't know, and it is everyone's task to do so, not just a job for the extroverts.

The Community strives for informality and participation in its liturgies – the opposite of all those formal church services in which none of the congregation plays any significant part. Comments and ad lib jokes during a service are not unusual with us – it does not seem to spoil the atmosphere, on the contrary – and newcomers are encouraged to join in fully with readings and intercessions and ritual. Wine, bread (home-baked when we can manage it), a bowl of sand with candles beside it, a plate for the collection, chairs in a circle with carpets for those who prefer to sit on the floor, are arranged in advance. The leader for the evening – we take it in turns – sits in the circle beside the other worshippers. Often she or he will have been responsible for preparing and copying a special liturgy, but if not then our prepared workbooks will be used. Readers for the lessons will have been chosen from the congregation; we aim to ask everyone to read, not just those who do it beautifully.

The leader will begin by welcoming everyone, asking people to introduce themselves by name, and explaining briefly the form the service will take. Large parts of the liturgy will be spoken by members of the Community (and everyone who is there is a member for that evening) either in unison, or going round and round the circle with one person at a time speaking. The intention is to make everyone feel included and equally valued.

At the end the leader will give out any information, will ask if there are any notices, and will invite worshippers to stay for a cup of tea.

## Opening

## Acclamations

FROM THE fragmented world of our everyday lives
We gather together in search of wholeness.
By many cares and preoccupations
by diverse and separate aims
are we separated from one another
and divided within ourselves.
Yet we know that no branch is utterly severed
From the Tree of life that sustains us all.

WE HAVE come together in this quiet space
to reflect upon our lives in the light of the Christian mystery.
To pray for ourselves and others.
To deepen the sense of affection and understanding we have for each
other, women for women, men for men, and women and men for one another.

1　O GOD, I seek you while you may be found;
2　I call upon you while you are near.
3　O God, you are my Redeemer,
　　abundant in forgiveness and love.
4　Your thoughts are not our thoughts,
　　neither are your ways our ways.
5　As the rain and the snow come down from the skies
　　and return not again but water the earth,
6　bringing forth life and giving growth,
　　seed for the sowing and bread for the eating;
7　so the Word that goes forth from your mouth
　　will not return to you empty,
8　but it will accomplish that which you purpose
　　and succeed in the task that you give it.

Be in love with life

**wrestle with the chaos and the pain**

with yourself and with others

**spirit echoing Spirit**

trusting in the victory of the vulnerable;

**glimpsing the peace,**

the wholeness,

**the spaciousness,**

the justice,

**and the joy
that comes from following the Pioneer**

made perfect in suffering;

**striving and yearning and crying out
from the very depths and heights
of the world's anguish and the world's bliss,**

and so becoming friends and partners of God
in the divine creating.

Be silent.
Be still.
Alone. Empty
before your God.
Say nothing.
Ask nothing.
Be silent.
Be still.
Let your God
look upon you.
That is all.
She knows.
She understands.
She loves you with
an enormous love.
She only wants to
look upon you
with her love.
Quiet.
Still.
Be.

Let your God –
Love you.

The living God,
The living, moving Spirit of God
has called us together –
in witness, in celebration, in struggle.

Reach out toward each other
(We all stand and hold hands)
Our God reaches out toward us.

Let us worship God.
(Drop hands)

IN THE beginning,
in the very beginning,
God gave birth to,
God delivered,
God created
the heavens and the earth.
Yes, out of the womb
of fertile divinity
emerged our mother,
the earth.

Mother earth, sister sea, giving birth, energy,
reaching out, touching me lovingly.

LOVING God,
together we seek the way,
helping, watching, learning, leading,
each step forging new links,
each dialogue opening further
the channels of peace and understanding.
We stand poised on the brink of greatness,
drawn by the Spirit into new realms of hope and trust.
The barriers of past centuries are slowly crumbling.
We pray that the skeletons of division and discord
will be laid to rest,
and that the people of God will be fully mobilized.
For these and all your mercies,
we thank and praise you O God.

## The Gloria

WE ADORE the glory and the truth that is God.
Everything within us utters praise.
Our being is formed for this purpose and no other.
All our loves and works find meaning in you.

Jesus, who shows us what God is like,
forgive us our failure to understand
but keep us in your dazzling presence.

For there we learn the nature of holiness
and partake with you in the secret of the godhead.

GLORY BE to you,   Ground of all Being,
Source of all Strength,
Giver of all Power.
Amen.

1   GLORY IN all my seeing
Glory in all my being
2   Glory in all my speaking
Glory in all my seeking
3   Glory in all my hearing
Glory in every appearing
4   Glory in all my feeling
Glory in God's revealing
5   Glory of the mighty Three
Glory entwining round me
6   Glory in the opening day
Glory in the rocky way
7   Glory in the morning light
Glory in the darkest night
8   Glory there for beholding
Glory ever me enfolding.

9   Glory of God
Hand above
10   Glory of Christ
Heart of love
11   Glory of Spirit
Covering dove.

Glory to God, glory to God,
glory to our maker.
Glory to God, glory to God,
glory to our maker.
To God be glory forever.
To God be glory forever.
Alleluia. Amen.
Alleluia. Amen.
Alleluia. Amen.
Alleluia. Amen.

Glory to Christ, glory to Christ,
glory to our brother.
Glory to Christ, glory to Christ,
glory to our brother.
To Christ be glory forever.
To Christ be glory forever.
Alleluia. Amen.
Alleluia. Amen.
Alleluia. Amen.
Alleluia. Amen.

Glory to God, glory to God,
glory to the Spirit.
Glory to God, glory to God,
glory to the Spirit.
Give us your freedom forever.
Give us your freedom forever.
Alleluia. Amen.
Alleluia. Amen.
Alleluia. Amen.
Alleluia. Amen.

Jesus, who was lost and found in the garden,
never to be lost again,
Stand by us in the darkness of our crucifixions,
as the women stood by you.
Die and rise with us in the suffering of the world.
Be reborn with us
as love and hope and faith and endurance
outlast cruelty and death. Amen.

## Collects

O God, the power of the powerless,
you have chosen as your witnesses
those whose voice is not heard.
Grant that, as women first announced
the Resurrection
though they were not believed,
we too may have courage
to persist in proclaiming your word,
In the power of Jesus Christ. Amen.

O God our deliverer,
you cast down the mighty,
and lift up those of no account;
as Elisabeth and Mary embraced
with songs of liberation,
so may we also be pregnant with your Spirit,
and affirm one another in hope for the world,
through Jesus Christ. Amen.

God of the outsider
who in your servant Ruth
established the line of our salvation;
give us her love and courage
with all the women who wait
like strangers in your church,
to travel a new path;
put our faith in the faith of a woman,
and boldly claim your promise,
through Jesus Christ. Amen.

God whose body is all creation,
may we come to know you in all the earth
and feel you in our blood;
so will no part of us, or the world,
be lost to your transforming grace.
Amen.

Flame-dancing Spirit, come
Sweep us off our feet and
Dance us through our days.
Surprise us with your rhythms;
Dare us to try new steps, explore
New patterns and new partnerships;
Release us from old routines
To swing in abandoned joy and
Fearful adventure. And
In the intervals,
Rest us
In your still centre. Amen.

Spirit of Truth
whom the world can never grasp,
touch our hearts
with the shock of your coming;
fill us with desire
for your disturbing peace;
and fire us with longing
to speak your uncontainable word,
through Jesus Christ. Amen.

Christ our healer,
beloved and remembered by women,
Speak to the grief which makes us forget,
and to the terror that makes us cling,
and give us back our name;
that we may greet you clearly
and proclaim your risen life. Amen.

God our deliverer
whose approaching birth still shakes
the foundations of our world,
may we so wait for your coming
with eagerness and hope
that we embrace without terror
the labour pangs of the new age,
through Jesus Christ. Amen.

Thanks be to God that we have risen this day
– To the rising of this life itself.

Be the purpose of God between us and each purpose.
The hand of God between us and each hand.
The pain of Christ between us and each pain.
The love of Christ between us and each love.

CHRIST, OUR only true light,
before whose bright cloud
your friends fell to the ground;
we bow before your cross
that we may remember in our bodies
the dead who fell like shadows;
and that we may refuse to be prostrated
before the false brightness
of any other light,
looking to your power alone
for hope of resurrection from the dead.
Amen.

O GRACIOUS God
You bring us together from many different places,
You endow us with varied gifts and responsibilities,
You challenge us to respond to your call.
Guide our halting, impatient steps,
Sustain us and help us sustain each other,
that, through our labours
We may help bring into the world
your sweet justice,
through Jesus our Redeemer. Amen.

LET THY Resurrection light radiate all our worship
by the power of the Holy Spirit.
Help us to know ourselves
as women and men who have been made new.
By that same power inspire us to walk
even as he walked;
that going on our way in faith and gladness
we may come at last to those things which eye hath not seen
nor ear heard
but which thou hast prepared for all them that truly love thee
from the beginning of the world. Amen.

GOD OUR mother,
you hold our life within you;
nourish us at your breast,
and teach us to walk alone.
Help us so to receive your tenderness
and respond to your challenge
that others may draw life from us,
in your name. Amen.

SPIRIT OF integrity,
you drive us out into the desert
to search out your truth.
Give us clarity to know what is right,
and courage to reject what is expedient;
that we may abandon the false innocence
of failing to choose at all;
but may follow the purposes of Jesus Christ.
Amen.

O CHRIST THE Risen Word,
raise us with you in this glorious Easter season.
Nurture the resurrection life in us.
Send your Spirit where the new season dances
and brings us into the full promise of Spring.
Amen.

THE WILDERNESS and the dry land shall be glad,
the desert shall rejoice and blossom;
like the crocus it shall blossom abundantly,
and rejoice with joy and singing.

For Christ the Word is living, being, spirit,
all things greening, all creativity.
This Word, now newly springing,
manifests itself in every creature.

Come then, my love,
my lovely one, come.
For lo, the winter is past,
the rain is over and gone.
Christ's springtime is among us and within us.

Christ is risen, our Springtime is come! Alleluia!

**Canticles**

As ONE WHO travels in the heat
longs for cool waters,
so do I yearn for wisdom;
and as one who is weary with walking
so shall I sit at her well and drink.

For her words are like streams in the desert;
she is like rain on parched ground,
like a fountain whose waters fail not.
Whoever hears her voice
will be content with nothing less;
and whoever drinks of her will long for more.

But who can find wisdom's dwelling place,
and who has searched her out?
for many have said to me, lo, here is wisdom,
and there you shall find understanding;

here is true worship of God,
and thus shall your soul be satisfied.

But there was no delight in my soul;
all my senses were held in check.
My body became alien to me,
and my heart was shrivelled within me.

For I sought understanding without justice;
discernment without the fear of God.
I would have filled my belly with the husks of knowledge,
and quenched my thirst with what was already stagnant.

But you have blessed me with emptiness, O God;
you have spared me to remain unsatisfied.
And now I yearn for justice;
like an infant that cries for the breast,
and cannot be pacified,
I hunger and thirst for oppression to be removed,
and to see the right prevail.

So while I live I will seek your wisdom, O God;
while I have strength to search, I will follow her ways.
For her words are like rivers in the desert;
she is like rain on parched ground,
like a fountain whose waters fail not.

Then shall my soul spring up like grass,
and my heart recover her greenness;
and from the deepest places of my soul
shall flow streams of living water.

## Confessions of Faith

WE BELIEVE in the presence of God in the world.

She is our mother, source of deep wisdom, who:
> holds and protects us,
> nourishes our bodies,
> comforts our pain,
> hears and accepts our times of failure and success.

She is our lover and is allowed to touch our pain:
> healing and recreating,
> seeking out what is hidden,
> revealing deep, precious mysteries.

She is our friend who stands alongside us:
> working co-operatively for the common good,
> sharing our concerns,
> fiercely criticizing our lack of integrity.

We believe in the presence of God in our world.
We meet her as people met her in Jesus, in countless relationships
which are at once human and divine:
> in simple encounters with men, women and children,
> in office and schoolroom, home and supermarket,
> in the community of her people.

We believe in the presence of God in our world,
whose truth is denied, in anguish, like that of Jesus on the cross,
whenever:
> food is withheld,
> the earth is poisoned, abused or destroyed,
> people are oppressed, denied dignity and responsibility,
> tortured or killed.

Together we affirm the truth and goodness of God, our mother, lover
and friend and commit ourselves to her in following the way of our
brother Jesus.

Leader    WE BELIEVE in God

All    Who created women and men in God's own image;
who created the world and gave both sexes the care of the earth.

Leader    We believe in Jesus

All    Child of God, chosen by God, born of the woman Mary;
who listened to women and stayed in their homes,
who looked for the kingdom with them,
who was followed and supported by women disciples.

Leader    We believe in Jesus

All    Who discussed theology with a woman at a well,
who received anointing from a woman at Simon's house,
and who rebuked the men guests who scorned her.

Leader    We believe in Jesus

All    Who healed a woman on the Sabbath,
who spoke of God as a woman seeking a lost coin –
as a woman who swept, seeking the lost.

Leader    We believe in Jesus

All    Who thought of pregnancy and birth with reverence.

Leader    We believe in Jesus

All    Who appeared first to Mary Magdalene,
and sent her with the message – 'Go and tell'.

Leader    We believe in the wholeness of God

All    In whom there is neither Jew nor Greek, slave nor free,
male nor female, for all are one in God.

Leader    We believe in the Holy Spirit

All    As she moves over the waters of creation, and over the earth;
the woman spirit of God, who created us and gave us birth
and covers us with her wings.

### The Drama of Creation

Leader  In the beginning, God made the world:
Women  Made it and mothered it,
Men  Shaped it and fathered it;
Women  Filled it with seed and with signs of fertility,
Men  Filled it with love and its folk with ability.
Leader  All that is green, blue, deep and growing,
All  God's is the hand that created you.
Leader  All that crawls, flies, swims, walks or is motionless,
All  God's is the hand that created you.
Leader  All that speaks, sings, cries, laughs or keeps silence,
All  God's is the hand that created you.
Leader  All that suffers, lacks, limps or longs for an end,
All  God's is the hand that created you.
Leader  The world belongs to the Lord,
All  The earth and its people are his.

### The Drama of the Incarnation

Leader  When the time was right, God sent the Son.
Women  Sent him and suckled him,
Men  Reared him and risked him;
Women  Filled him with laughter and tears and compassion,
Men  Filled him with anger and love and devotion.
Leader  Unwelcomed child, refugee and runaway,
All  Christ is God's own son.
Leader  Skilled tradesman and redundant carpenter,
All  Christ is God's own son.
Leader  Feeder and teacher, healer and antagonist,
All  Christ is God's own son.
Leader  Lover of the unlovable, toucher of the untouchable, forgiver of the unforgivable,
All  Christ is God's own son.
Leader  Loved by women, feared by men; befriended by the weak, despised by the strong; deserted by his listeners, denied by his friends; bone of our bone, flesh of our flesh, writing heaven's pardon over earth's mistakes.
All  Christ is God's own son.
Leader  The Word became flesh,
All  He lived among us, he was one of us.

We believe in God
        Maker, Redeemer and Sustainer of Life
        without beginning or end.
        whose life-giving love was let loose on the first Easter Sunday
        and whose life-giving love we share and proclaim here today.

We believe in God
        who gave up the divine life and submitted to the darkness
        and terror of the grave
        and who enters with us into every darkness and terror we
        shall ever face.

We believe in God
        who raised Christ from the death of the grave to glorious
        new life
        and who raises our lives from sin and despair to newness
        and hope again.

We believe in God
        who met the grief-stricken Mary in the garden and called her
        into hope by the uttering of her name.
        and who meets us in our grief and gives us courage to hope
        again by tenderly calling our name.

We believe in God
        who sent Mary out from the garden to be the witness and
        apostle of the resurrection
        and who commissions us, like Mary, to be bearers of hope
        and good news in our world.

We believe in God
        Maker, Redeemer and Sustainer of Life.
        without beginning or end,
        whose life-giving love was let loose on the first Easter Sunday
        and whose life-giving love we share and proclaim today
        to all women and men, wherever and whoever they are,
        loved, blessed and called by God,
        without beginning or end.

## Discussion

There are usually two, and sometimes, three, readings at St Hilda's services, often taken from the lectionary of the Alternative Service Book. Sometimes one or two are taken from other sources, poetry, news stories, or other material. When they are finished there is a silence and then anyone present may comment. At times it may be a good idea to suggest that no one speaks more than once, and to restrict the discussion to a certain length of time, say ten minutes. If there is a large number of people it may be better to divide into small groups.

## Intercessions

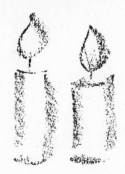

At every St Hilda's service there is a bowl of sand with one large candle burning in the middle of it, and a basket with small candles standing beside it. At the time of the intercessions we sit in silence for five to ten minutes. When they wish, worshippers get up, light a small candle from the bigger one, and place it beside it in the sand, saying 'I light this candle for . . .' naming their purpose e.g. the homeless, the hungry, X who is ill, Y who is dying, A and B who are going through a bad time in their marriage. Or they may say 'I light this candle in gratitude for . . .' e.g. an illness they have recovered from, some good event in their lives, etc. Or they may prefer to light the candle in silence.

Sometimes alternatively a lighted candle is passed from one person to another, with each naming their subject of intercession when the candle is handed to them, or simply holding the candle for a moment before passing it on.

I LIGHT the candle,
the light shines out,
the candle is transformed,
the spirit gives of herself,
we all receive.


SISTERS AND brothers of the Community of St Hilda,
Apart and part of the whole,
In isolation and in communion,
Near and far,
Together we pray:

Heal us, Creator God, that we may become whole;
Inspire us, Spirit of God, and instil in us new wisdom;
Lead us, brother Jesus, to love and serve each other;
Defeating the fears which lead to discrimination;
Affirming all women and men as celebrants in the eucharist of life.

God of justice and peace, you stand with those who are poor,
You ask us to be the voice of the voiceless.
We call upon you for those who have suffered the injustice
of war and greed, from the depths of our being we cry to you:

Creator God, you know what we need, without our words.
Hear our prayer and hear also our silence. Grant us those
things we cannot or dare not voice. We make these prayers
through our brother Jesus. Amen.

| | | | |
|---|---|---|---|
| 1 | Into your hands, Lord, | | |
| 2 | This solitude, | | |
| 3 | Into your hands, Lord, | | |
| 4 | This emptiness. | | |
| 5 | Into your hands, Lord | | |
| 6 | This loneliness. | | |
| 7 | Into your hands, – | All | From the flowing of the tide |
| 8 | This all. | | to its ebbing |
| 9 | Into your hands, O Lord, | | From the waxing of life |
| 10 | This grief. | | to its waning |
| 11 | Into your hands, | | |
| 12 | This sleeping fear. | 1 | Of your Peace provide us |
| All | Into your hands, O Lord – | 2 | Of your Light lead us |
| | What is left, | 3 | Of your Goodness give us |
| | What is left | 4 | Of your Grace grant us |
| | Of me. | 5 | Of your Power protect us |
| | | 6 | Of your Love lift us |
| | | All | And in your arms accept us |
| | | | From the ebbing of the tide |
| | | | to its flowing |
| | | | From the waning of life |
| | | | to its waxing. |

**Litany**

FOR THE darkness of waiting
of not knowing what is to come
of staying ready and quiet and attentive,
we praise you O God.

**For the darkness and the light
are both alike to you**

For the darkness of staying silent
for the terror of having nothing to say
and for the greater terror
of needing to say nothing,
we praise you O God.

**For the darkness and the light
are both alike to you**

For the darkness of loving
in which it is safe to surrender
to let go of our self-protection
and to stop holding back our desire,
we praise you, O God.

**For the darkness and the light
are both alike to you**

For the darkness of choosing
when you give us the moment
to speak, and act, and change,
and we cannot know what we have set
in motion,
but we still have to take the risk,
we praise you O God.

**For the darkness and the light
are both alike to you**

For the darkness of hoping
in a world which longs for you,
for the wrestling and the labouring of
all creation
for wholeness and justice and freedom,
we praise you O God.

**For the darkness and the light
are both alike to you**

BLESSING THE BREAD
(a litany for four voices)

1 IN THE beginning was God
2 In the beginning, the source of
all that is.
3 In the beginning, God yearning
4 God, moaning
1 God, labouring
2 God, giving birth
3 God, rejoicing
4 And God loved what she
had made
1 And God said, 'It is good'.

2 Then God, knowing that all
that is good is shared
3 Held the earth tenderly in
her arms.
4 God yearned for relationship.
1 God longed to share the
good earth.
2 And humanity was born in the
yearning of God.
3 We were born to share the earth.

4 In the earth was the seed
1 In the earth was the grain
2 In the grain was the harvest
3 In the harvest was the bread
4 In the bread was the power.

1 And God said, All shall eat
of the earth
2 All shall eat of the seed.
3 All shall eat of the grain
4 All shall eat of the harvest.
1 All shall eat of the bread.
2 All shall eat of the power.
3 God said, You are my people
4 My friends,
1 My lovers,
2 My sisters,
3 And brothers,
4 All of you shall eat
1 Of the bread
2 And the power
3 All shall eat

4 Then God, gathering up her
courage in love, said,

1 Let there be bread!
2 And God's sisters, her friends
and lovers, knelt on the earth
3 planted the seeds
4 prayed for the rain
1 sang for the grain
2 made the harvest
3 cracked the wheat
4 pounded the corn
1 kneaded the dough
2 kindled the fire
3 filled the air with the smell
of fresh bread
4 And there was bread!
1 And it was good!

2 We, the sisters of God, say today
3 All shall eat of the bread,

4 And the power,
1 We say today,
2 All shall have power
3 And bread,
4 Today we say
1 Let there be bread.
2 And let there be power!
3 Let us eat of the bread and
the power!
4 And all will be filled
1 For the bread is rising!

2 By the power of God
3 Women are blessed,
4 By the women of God
1 The bread is blessed
2 By the bread of God
3 the power is blessed
4 By the power of bread
1 the power of women
2 the power of God
3 The people are blessed.

All The earth is blessed
And the bread is rising.

## Forms of
## Confession

WE NEED YOUR forgiveness, merciful God,
For not allowing our complacency to be shattered,
For taking refuge too often in the familiar and the certain;
For not believing in the victory of vulnerability,
For not daring to accept your gifts nor claim your promises.
Grant us true repentance.
Set us free to hear your word to us.
Set us free to serve you.

I DENY God's gifts in me
and I deny God's gifts in others.
I ask forgiveness.

God forgives you. Forgive yourself. Be at peace.

O GOD, WE bring you our failure,
our hunger, our disappointment, our despair,
our greed, our aloofness, our loneliness.
When we cling to others in desperation
Or turn from them in fear
Strengthen us in love.
Teach us, women and men
To use our power with care.

We turn to you, O God,
We renounce evil,
We claim your love,
We choose to be made whole.

All   GOD, YOU know us as we are;
you know our selfishness,
our anger and bitterness,
our fear and apathy,
our hardness of heart,
our deliberate blindness,
our need to begin again.

Leader   In your mercy and love,

All   Forgive us, change and renew us.

Keeper and Companion of us all, forgive us.

You call us, like Eve, to co-create new worlds;
But we turn away and backslide into the comfortable or the certain.

You call us, like Miriam, to dance for freedom;
But we turn away and glory in how far we have come, forgetting how
far we have to go.

You call us, like Deborah, to judge our world, to make decisions and
offer counsel;
But we turn away and apologise for our anger and compromise our
positions.

You call us, like Naomi and Ruth, to love one another;
But we turn away and compete, taking vengeance on those most
like ourselves.

You call us, like Mary, to be faithful bearers of your word;
But we turn away and strive to become perfectionists.

You call us, like Thecla and Phoebe, to begin a new church;
But we turn away and accept a place in the system, rationalizing
things the way they are.

Merciful Healer, we do not claim our gifts. We do not face up to
your call. We do not appreciate your partnership in creating a new
community and a new world. Today we repent. We turn from our old
ways and commit ourselves to new partnerships for holding on and to
new visions for a different heaven and earth.

Leader  I will pour clean water upon you,
        says God, our mother,
        and you shall be clean
        from all your uncleanness;
        from all your idols I will cleanse you. (Ez. 36:25)

All     Wash away my guilt, O God,
        and cleanse me from my sin. (Ps. 51:2)

Leader  Let us call to mind a particular failing
        which we would like to have washed away.


1    God of love and forgiveness
     Save us by your tenderness
2    From each deed of evilness
3    From each act of sinfulness
4    From each thought of carelessness
5    From each idea of wickedness
6    From each word of hurtfulness
7    From each speech of harmfulness

All  Save us by your tenderness
     God of love and forgiveness.

## Absolution

The person presiding at the service turns to the person on her/his left and makes the sign of the cross on their forehead, saying 'God forgives you. Forgive others. Forgive yourself' or one of the similar forms given here. That person in turn passes the absolution to the person on her/his left. Sometimes oil is used to make the sign of the cross, and sometimes, alternatively to the above, we wash and dry the hands of the person sitting next to us.

GOD forgives you
Forgive others
Forgive yourself

BE healed, be whole.

WOMAN/Man, your sins are forgiven,
Go in peace.

At the time of the Peace we get up from the circle and walk around touching or embracing one another. The Peace is usually the time we place money in the Offertory bowl.

## The Peace

BROTHER/Sister, be at peace.

PEACE I leave with you,
My own peace I give to you.

May Christ's peace invade, flood and shake the foundations of our hearts and lives, in this Community, in our daily lives, in our witness to the world; let peace BREAK OUT!

PEACE AND love are always alive in us, but we are not always alive to peace and love.

PEACE IS flowing like a river, flowing out through you and me
Spreading out into the desert, setting all the captives free.

Love is flowing like a river. . . .

Joy is flowing like a river. . . .

Hope is flowing like a river. . . .

WE MEET together to share this meal,
may it express our love for one another
our commitment to each other
and point us beyond ourselves
to the needs of the world.

The peace of God be with you all.

**And also with you.**

AND OUR approach was in peace,
And we were established in the Spirit of unity.

GOD MAKES peace within us.
Let us claim it.
God makes peace between us.
let us share it.

WE HOLD UP our smallness to your greatness,
our fear to your love.
Our tiny act of giving to your great generosity
Ourselves to you.

## The Offertory

GOD BE with you
And with your spirit.
We turn our faces to God
we offer our hearts.

WE COME with offerings – of our time,
our money, our strength,
our pleasure in one another's company.
All these we bring to God in dedication,
and for use in the glory of the realm of God.

As each person brings the offerings of bread, wine, water and a candle, all say:

The bread    THE BREAD we bring, is it not a sharing of the
Body of Christ?

The wine    The cup of blessing which we bring, is it not a sharing
of the Blood of Christ?

The water    God our Mother, you wash us and cleanse us and
come among us as One who serves.

The candle    In the beginning, when it was very dark, God said,
Let there be light.

GOD, WHO cares for us,
The wonder of whose presence fills us with awe.
Let kindness, justice and love shine in our world.
Let your secrets be known here as they are in heaven.
Give us the food and the hope we need for today.
Forgive us our wrongdoing
as we forgive the wrongs done to us.
Protect us from pride and from despair
and from the fear and hate which can swallow us up.
In you is truth, meaning, glory and power,
while words come and go. Amen.

## Prayer of Jesus

BELOVED,
our Father and Mother,
in whom is heaven.
Hallowed be your name,
followed be your royal way,
done be your will and rule,
throughout the whole creation.
With the bread we need for today,
feed us,
In the hurts we absorb from one another,
forgive us.
In times of temptation and test,
strengthen us.
From trials too great to endure,
spare us.
From the grip of all that is evil,
free us.
For you reign in the glory
of the power that is love,
now and forever. Amen.

GOD, LOVER of us all, most holy one,
help us to respond to you,
to create what you want for us here on earth.
Give us today enough for our needs;
forgive our weak and deliberate offences,
just as we must forgive others when they hurt us.
Help us to resist evil and to do what is good;
for we are yours,
endowed with your power to make us whole.
Amen.

## Agape

Be GENTLE when you touch bread;
let it not lie uncared for, unwanted.
So often bread is taken for granted.
There is such beauty in bread –
beauty of sun and soil,
beauty of patient toil.
Wind and rain have caressed it.
Christ often blessed it.
So let us be gentle in touching bread.

Keep sober when you drink wine.
Let it not be wasted or taken in vain,
nor like water washed down a drain.
There is the deepest art in the creation of wine.
Choice of the right soil;
skill in dressing the vine
judgement of the right time of harvest;
craft of transforming the grapes into wine.
Christ saw it poured out and spilt as his blood.
Let wine not be misunderstood.

I am quiet now before God
As a child lies quietly in its mothers' arms
As a child that lies quiet is my soul. (Ps. 131:2)

As WOMEN bake bread and share it with their families,
I break my bread to share with you.

**In God's new world we share the Bread of Life.**

As women shed their blood to give you life,
I shed my blood to give you a new life.

**In God's new world we share the Wine of Heaven.**

Bread   Broken for us

Wine   Poured out for us

Christ   Dying and living for us.

O LIVING Bread from Heaven,
Jesu, our Saviour good,
who your own self hast given
to be our soul's true food.
For us your body broken
hung on the cross of shame.
This bread its hallowed token
we break in your true name.

O Stream of Love Unending
poured from the one true Vine,
with our weak nature blending
the strength of life divine.
Our thankful faith confessing
in thy life-blood outpoured.
We drink this cup of blessing
and praise your name, O Lord.

Today we share bread and wine together
as a sign that we are one humanity,
as a pledge that we will work for justice,
as a foretaste of that which can be
despite what is and what has been.
May the Holy Spirit that guides us all
be present in this feast,
taking this bread and wine,
the concerns that we have expressed,
the lives that we lead,
and transforming them all
for the unity of humankind
and the service of love.

Blessed be the Eternal Sustainer.
Working with soil and elements and human toil.
Bringing forth bread from the earth.

**When the bodies of others are broken,
we are broken.**

Blessed be the Eternal Sustainer.
Working with soil and elements and human toil.
Making the fruit of the vine.

**We are all one kin, one blood.
When the blood of others spills, our blood
is spilled.**

Come, let us celebrate the supper of Jesus.
Let us make a huge loaf of bread and let us bring
abundant wine.

**Because today we celebrate our meeting with Jesus.
Today we renew our commitment to the kingdom.
Nobody will be hungry.**

When we break bread together,
do we not share in the Body of Christ?

**We seek to share your life, gracious God.**

When we take the cup,
do we not share in the life-blood of Christ?

**We seek to share your life, gracious God.**

Be present, be present,
even though we are unworthy for you to come
to us.
Only your peaceful presence
can nourish us in faith,
bind us together in love
and fill us with hope.
So that we might share in your service. Amen.

With bread and wine, the signs of God's passion,
　　　— let us celebrate the passion of God's own heart
　　　— let us remember the passion of the world
　　　— and let us offer the passion of our hearts.

## 1  God is with us.

**Her Spirit is here.**

**The Eucharist**

Lift up your hearts.

**We lift them up to God.**

Let us give thanks to our Inspirator.

**It is right to offer her thanks and praise.**

Spirit of God, who breathes fire into our very existence, filling us with heavenly joy and holy indignation at the plight of our world.
We worship you, we praise you, we recognize the symbol of your presence, your promise of solidarity with us on our journey.

We claim the sign of renewal given to a broken and discouraged community, now as then in Jerusalem.
For you came to your own, filling them with confidence, gusting through their lives, bringing ecstasy and wholeness, clarity and vision, hope and peace.
You enlightened their existence,
Enabled their mission,
Empowered them to be disciples of your word.

So, with all the women who followed you through your ministry, who watched you die and rise again,
and with all those who inspired and supported the early Church,
with Tabitha who showed solidarity with the poor,
Lydia who welcomed the tired and travel weary
and Priscilla who knew the meaning of persecution,
we praise you, singing:

**Holy, Holy,
God of all power!
Heaven and earth are full of your glory.
Come and deliver us, come and deliver us, come and deliver us,
God most high.**

66

**Blessed is One who comes in the name of our God!**
**Come and deliver us, come and deliver us, come and deliver us,**
**God most high.**

Blessed is Christ our brother,
who fills us with a sense of being one people, one community.
On the night he was betrayed,
he took bread, gave thanks, and broke it, saying:
'This is my body, which is given for you. Do this to remember me.'
In the same way, after supper he took the cup, blessed it and said:
'This cup is the new covenant made in my blood.
Do this whenever you drink it to remember me.'

**Christ has died.**
**Christ is risen.**
**Christ will come again.**

As one community we rejoice in your gifts,
we accept responsibility for our world;
we trust in your Spirit of challenge;
we welcome your presence in this bread and wine.
Drunk with longing for your deep and disturbing presence to be revealed to us, we praise
you with all who have derived inspiration from this story of renewal and refreshment.

Come now, pour your Spirit on us so we are better able to
proclaim your message,
see new visions,
dream new dreams.

In the name of Christ.

**Through him, with him, in him,**
**In the unity of the Holy Spirit,**
**All honour and glory be given to you,**
**O God our Source and Inspiration,**
**Now and forever.**
**Amen.**

Take and eat, for the peace of all nations.

Take and drink, for the love of all people.

**For you have shown us the path that leads to life.
And this feast will fill us with joy.**

2   MAY GOD be with you

**And also with you.**

Lift up your hearts.

**We lift them to our God.**

Let us adore and exalt our God.

**It is right to give our thanks and praise.**

O Eternal Wisdom,
We praise you and give you thanks,
because the beauty of death could not contain you.
You broke forth from the comfort of the grave;
before you the stone was moved,
and the tomb of our world was opened wide.
For on this day you were raised in power
and revealed yourself to women
as a beloved stranger,
offering for the rituals of the dead
the terror of new life
and of desire fulfilled.

Therefore, with the woman who gave you birth,
the women who befriended you and fed you;
who argued with you and touched you;
the women who anointed you for death;

the women who met you, risen from the dead;
and with all your lovers throughout the ages,
we praise you, singing:

Holy, holy

**Holy, holy**

God of all power,

**God of all power.**

Heaven and earth are full of your glory,

**Heaven and earth are full of your glory.**

Come and deliver us, come and deliver us, come and deliver us,
God most high.

**Come and deliver us, come and deliver us, come and deliver us,
God most high.**

Blest is one who comes in the name of our God.

**Blest is one who comes in the name of our God.**

Come and deliver us, come and deliver us, come and deliver us,
God most high.

**Come and deliver us, come and deliver us, come and deliver us,
God most high.**

Blessed is our brother Jesus,
who walks with us the road of our grief,
and is known again in the breaking of bread;
who, on the night he was handed over,
took bread, gave thanks, broke it, and said:

'This is my body, which is for you.
Do this to remember me.'
In the same way also the cup, after supper, saying:
'This cup is the new covenant in my blood.
Do this whenever you drink it,
to remember me.'

**Christ has died.**
**Christ is risen.**
**Christ will come again.**

Come now, disturbing spirit of our God,
breathe on these bodily things
and make us one body in Christ.
Open our graves, unbind our eyes,
and name us here;
touch and heal all that has been buried in us,
that we need not cling to our pain,
but may go forth with power
to release resurrection in the world.

3   O God, our Father and our Mother
The God who is and was and will be
before and beyond our little lives.
Who made all that is.
And who is known to us in our own hearts
And in the lives of others.

We come once more to trace the pattern
of death and resurrection
that is written throughout our world.

With the saints and ancestors
we behold that mystery
and beholding it adore you.

(Singing)  **Holy, Holy, God of all power.**
**Heaven and earth are full of your glory.**
**Come and deliver us, come and deliver us, come and deliver us,**
**God most High.**

**Blessed is One who comes in the name of our God.**
**Come and deliver us, come and deliver us, come and deliver us,**
**God most High.**

At Easter we are close to the agony of Good Friday.
To the terrible humiliation of Jesus.
Scourged and crucified;
mocked and driven out,
as your children are hurt and humiliated still.

Yet that same agony flowered in joy.
The flower grew in the dark of the tomb
and burst apart the rock.
In taking bread and wine,
touching, breaking, pouring, drinking,
we know that we enter the holiest mystery
and that by doing so our hearts will be changed.

Jesus, on the night of betrayal, took bread,
he gave thanks for it and broke it
and gave it to his friends, saying:
'Take and eat. This is my own body which
I surrender because of you.
Do the same action to remember me.'

Then, after supper, he picked up the cup of wine.
he gave thanks for that and passed it around,
saying, 'Everyone drink of this.
This is my blood witnessing to a new understanding;
I spill it for you and for many more to cure the
wounds of the spirit and to take away ignorance.
When you eat together, drink like this,
and remember what I say.'

At Easter, as at every Eucharist, we recall the days of
Jesus' Passion with wonder and love.
We ask you, God creator, to enter this action so that our
hearts are moved to loving, and our fear and spite fade away.
We only partly understand what we do, and we ask you to
fill out our intention to fulfil your divine purpose,
that all who partake of this Easter feast may be
completed in grace.

Glory be to you, and may a glimpse of that glory
be allowed to us.

President   (Breaking the bread)

In breaking this bread and sharing it
We share in the death of Jesus, the pain of the world,
the hope of resurrection.

All   **And by partaking we become one body.**

President   In pouring this wine and sharing it
We enter into the passion of Jesus,
the blood shed in the world,
and the hope of resurrection.

All   **By drinking we become one body.**

4   WE take bread
symbol of labour – exploited, degraded.
symbol of life.

**Life for us.**

We will break the bread
because Christ the source of life
was broken for the exploited and downtrodden.

**Broken for us.**

We take wine
symbol of blood spilt in war and conflict
symbol of new life.

**Poured out for us.**

We will drink the wine
because Christ the peace of the world
was killed by violence.

**Because of us.**

Now bread and wine are before us;
the memory of our meals;
our working;
our talking;
our loving.
Before us the depths of our life.

**Thanks be to God.**

The Spirit of God be with you

**And also with you.**

Lift up your hearts.

**We lift them up to God.**

Let us give thanks to God.

**It is right to offer thanks and praise.**

We give thanks for the history of God's people;
the defiance of the prophet
in startling and angry tongue,
in lonely dispute
and long, tiring conflict.

**Thanks be to God.**

For Jesus of Nazareth
living the truth of God
and the truth of us.
Bringing good news to the poor,
liberation for the oppressed
and for all down the ages
who have lived Jesus' story.

**Thanks be to God.**

For the promptings of the Spirit.
For all we know of ourselves;
the story that shapes us,
the grieving and the pain,
the oppressor that lies deep in our own soul,
the seeking and the loving.

**Thanks be to God.**

For all that binds us together in our humanity,
with all who live and have lived,
who have cried and are crying,
who hunger and are thirsty,
who pine for justice
and who sing and pray for the coming of God's kingdom.

Holy, Holy,

**Holy, Holy,**

God of all power,

**God of all power.**

Heaven and earth are full of your glory,

**Heaven and earth are full of your glory.**

Come and deliver us, come and deliver us, come and deliver us,
God most High.

**Come and deliver us, come and deliver us, come and deliver us,
God most High.**

Blest is One who comes in the name of our God.

**Blest is One who comes in the name of our God.**

Come and deliver us, come and deliver us, come and deliver us,
God most High.

**Come and deliver us, come and deliver us, come and deliver us,
God most High.**

We are bound to each other
and with all people
regardless of sex, race or class.
And in this we are bound to Jesus
who, in the same night that he was handed over
to torture and execution
took bread and gave you thanks,
he broke it and gave it to his friends, saying:
**Take, eat, this is my body, my living presence, given for you;
do this to re-member me.**

In the same way he took the cup of wine
and gave you thanks and gave it to them, saying:
**Drink this all of you; for this is my blood, my very life;
spent for you; do this to re-member me.**

We eat this food to bring us together.
We drink this wine to bring us alive in the world.

**This is the death we celebrate.**
**This is the new life we proclaim.**
**This is the vision we live.**

So we are joined with all who labour for justice;
with all women and men of faith;
with all who share our love of Jesus,
and those who seek truth and liberty in different ways.
We live and grow together
and we keep alive the memory of Jesus and his cross.
We awaken our hope in the resurrection,
in the new life where injustice lies defeated.

**Strengthen us, O God.**

We pray together that in eating the bread
and drinking the wine
our life will be enriched
and we make, here and now,
the new age a reality.

**Amen.**

We break this bread recalling the body of Christ broken for us.

**Help us to accept the cost of discipleship
and to take the risk of faith.**

The bread and wine are shared amongst the community, with the words:

**The body of Christ, broken for you.**

**The blood of Christ, shed for you.**

5    LET us give thanks.

**For all that is good.**

Let us give thanks
for the continuity of the universe;
for the sun rising day by day,
and the moon rising night by night;

for all the life with which we share this planet;
for the interactions and connections that bind us to it,
and the elements of which all is composed.

Let us give thanks.

**And seek to live in harmony with all about us.**

Let us give thanks
for the flow of human history;
for the events that have shaped and moulded us
and all our sisters and brothers;
for those who question that history;
for those who unearth the stories of the vanquished,
the oppressed, the forgotten, the unrecorded.

Let us give thanks.

**And take our place in the human story,
struggling for the unity of humankind.**

Let us give thanks
for those who have provided inspiration and hope;
for prophets and martyrs and poets;
thinkers and preachers and healers;
for those who have linked thought and action;
for reformers and rebels and strikers.

Let us give thanks.

**And join with them in the quest for justice.**

Let us give thanks
for all who have revealed or discovered deep and lasting truths;
let us celebrate their lives and deaths,
their thoughts and writings,
their continuing witness in the world today.

Let us give thanks.

**And share in spreading this prophetic vision.**

Today we give thanks for Jesus of Nazareth,
in whom Christians believe that God was especially present,
one of the channels through which God was made known to humanity.
On the night that he was betrayed, he feasted with his followers;
he took bread, gave thanks, broke it
and gave it to his disciples, saying,
'Take this and eat it.
This is my body broken for you.
Do this in remembrance of me'.

In the same way, after supper,
he took the cup of wine, gave thanks,
and gave it to them, saying,
'Drink from it all of you.
This is my blood of the new covenant,
poured out for you and for many.
Do this whenever you drink it
in remembrance of me'.

For all that Jesus of Nazareth means to us.

**We give thanks.**

So today we share bread and wine together
as a sign that we are one humanity,
as a pledge that we will work for justice,
as a foretaste of that which can be
despite what is and what has been.
May the Spirit that guides us all
be present in this feast,
taking this bread and wine,
the concerns that we have expressed,
the lives that we lead,
and transforming them all
for the unity of all creation
and the service of love.

God, whose body is all creation,
may we come to know you in all the earth
and feel you in our blood.
So will no part of us, or the world,
be lost to your transforming grace.

Alleluia! This living bread is broken
for the life of the world.

**Alleluia! Let us keep the feast.**    *break bread —*

*MLS — wine*

*(Share)*

*MLS — prayer*

## Post Communion

WHEN people turn
from the table
where bread is broken
and candles glow,
be sure you have invited them
not to your house
but to their own,
and offered not your wisdom
but your love.

THE FEAST is ended; depart in peace.
The work of the world lies before us.
Accomplish justice, with grace.

LET US go out in peace and in power.
**To love and serve the Lord.**

THOSE WHO work for change suffer resistance.

**So make us strong.**

Those who do new things sometimes feel afraid.

**So make us brave.**

Those who challenge the world as it is arouse anger.

**So grant us inner peace.**

Those who live joyfully are envied.

**So make us generous.**

Those who try to love encounter hate.

**So make us steadfast in you.**

The blessing of the God of Sarah and Hagar, as of Abraham
The blessing of Jesus born of the woman Mary.
The blessing of the Holy Spirit who broods over us
as a mother over her children,
Be with us now and forever. Amen.

**Blessing**

May the God who dances in creation,
who embraces us with human love,
who shakes our lives like thunder,
bless us and drive us out with power
to fill the world with her justice. Amen.

May the power and the mystery go before us, to show us the way,
shine above us to lighten our world,
lie beneath us to bear us up,
walk with us and give us companionship,
and glow and flow within us to bring us joy. Amen.

May Holy Wisdom,
kind to humanity,
steadfast, sure and free,
the breath of the power of God;
may she who makes all things new, in every age,
enter our souls,
and make us friends of God,
through Jesus Christ. Amen.

The blessing of God,
The eternal goodwill of God,
The shalom of God,
The wildness and the warmth of God,
be among us and between us
Now and always. Amen.

Now may every living being,
Young or old,
Living near or far,
Known to us or unknown,
Living, departed or yet to be born,
may every living being
be full of bliss. Amen.

## Palm Sunday Rite

THIS, THE springtime of the year, is the season of new birth and re-creation. This is also the week of the passion and death of our brother Jesus.

We strip these branches of the buds of new birth, as we recall the divesting of Jesus in his passion.
(Please remove a bud from the branch passed to you.)

And as we are left with these torn and bare branches, we bring before God, the creator of all, the destruction and disfigurement of so much of that creation.
(The bare branches are brought to the centre, and crosses formed.)

We stand in silence and repentance for our share in the sin of the world.

We use traditional hymns and carols, Taizé chants, and sometimes other chants e.g. Peruvian taught us by members. We are beginning to think about making up dances to music we particularly enjoy, but have not got very far in writing our own hymns.

## Music

Rage, wisdom, and our lives inflame
so living never rests the same:
you are creative power and art
to blow our mind and wrack our heart.

As fiery gale, as storm of love,
discomfort, burn, all wrong remove,
exposing with your searing light
the lovelessness we keep from sight.

Disrupt and right our unjust ways
With the abrasion of your grace,
while we're your foes let no rest come
till to Christ's love you've brought us home.

You gust and burn through time and space,
and strange your beauty, fierce your face;
disturb our sleep and break our peace;
till Christ's love win, don't, Lady, cease.

Bring us to love the Father, Son,
and you with them in love as one,
that through the ages all along
this may be our endless song:

Praise to love's eternal merit,
Father, Son and wisest Spirit.

vige, creatrix sophia
cordas tuorum inflamma
tu artis vis et studiae,
mentium es turbatio.

ventus amoris ignifer
mala combure omnia;
lumen adurens eluce
nostra detegens odia.

rumpe omnem iniuriam
asperitate gratiae;
dum hostes sumus oppugna
donec nos Christo tradamur.

pulchra tu fera domina,
et flas ubique flagranter;
somnum et pacem deportans
Christi nos implens amore.

doce nos te agnoscere
cum patri et cum filio
in caritate coniunctam
et nobis delectatio,

JUBILATE Deo, Jubilate Deo, Alleluia.

YOU CAN'T kill the spirit
She is like a mountain
Old and strong
She goes on and on.

O LORD, hear my prayer, O Lord hear my prayer;
When I call answer me.
O Lord hear my prayer, O Lord hear my prayer;
Come and listen to me.

UBI caritas et amor
Ubi caritas
Deus ibi est.

BLESS the Lord, my soul,
and bless his holy name.
Bless the Lord, my soul,
he leads me into life.

YOU SHALL go out with joy
and be led forth with peace,
and the mountains and the hills shall break forth before you.
There will be shouts of joy
and the trees of the field
shall clap, shall clap their hands.

And the trees of the field shall clap their hands,
and the trees of the field shall clap their hands,
and the trees of the field shall clap their hands,
and you'll go out with joy.

For all the saints who from their labours rest,
Who in the world their faith in God confessed,
Your name, O Jesus, be forever blessed.
Alleluia! Alleluia!

You were the Stranger in the dark of night,
With whom they strove to find their one true light,
To whom you gave God's blessing, ever bright.
Alleluia! Alleluia!

They are the folk who gave with love divine,
Always in service did their wills incline,
Forgetting self, they did with glory shine.
Alleluia! Alleluia!

They followed you, cast out the city's gate,
Killed by the eyes and guns of human hate,
Yet trumpets sound their resurrection fete.
Alleluia! Alleluia!

And there will dawn a yet more marvellous day,
The saints with laughter sing and dance and play,
The Clown of Glory tumbles in the Way.
Alleluia! Alleluia!

The group gathers in corporate silence to celebrate the Eucharist.

Such quietness means we must use our non-verbal ways of communicating with God and with each other. Where we would normally use words to pray and meditate, on this occasion we will use silence and bodily prayer gestures. If you are in doubt as to what is meant by a particular instruction, just look at what the celebrant is doing. In order for this type of contemplative Eucharist to be effective, it requires *total silence* on the part of all participants. Please respect this prayer attitude.

## Silent Eucharist

**Kyrie**  Opening Gestures for everyone: while *silently* saying *Kyrie Eleison* touch your hand to your head, then to your heart, then touch the earth (the floor). Repeat for *Christe Eleison*, and repeat again for *Kyrie Eleison*.

Next, stay bending over and use your hands as though you were sweeping up a mess from the floor, gather together any rubbish from your own inner life that you wish to throw away. Collect your imaginary pile in front of you. Now become aware of others around you, as together everyone lifts these piles high above their heads and throws them out into the cosmos for God to receive and cleanse them.

Repeat the ingathering of rubbish a second time. This time you are collecting the daily rubbish in your outward, everyday life and relationships. Again make individual piles. Become aware of the rest of the group and together lift them up to God.

Repeat the gestures one last time, bringing together the total rubbish of humanity in small piles, then raise them together to God.

**Collect for the day**  In prayer gesture bring your arms out to the side, palms up, then move them in a circle gesture until the palms touch [as if you were holding a beach ball]. Then bring your hands down to heart level so that the whole of your palms are touching together with thumbs inward and little fingers outward.

Pray your own collect for this day.

**Meditation**  The meditation is silent and could last 5–15 minutes.

A bell will open the meditation. Spend the time until you hear the bell again allowing God to speak to you. Centre yourself, relax, taking slow deep breaths. Now try to discern any sense of God by seeing if any one particular word or phrase comes to your mind. Stay with that word now.

When the bell rings, drop the word into any prayer you would now like to make. This may be for your own needs or for those of others. Use that word in your petitions or intercessions.

When the bell rings, drop the word altogether and just try to remain in the silence without any words or thoughts.

When the bell rings for the fourth time, open your eyes and begin to focus on the group again.

Intercessions    There is a bowl of sand with a lighted candle in the centre of the group. You are invited to light a small candle and place it in the sand, naming your petition silently within you.

Confession    Kneeling, raise your arms above your head and bring them straight down in front of you. Bending at the waist, bow to the floor so that your palms are touching the ground. This gesture is repeated three times. Each time pause to reflect before coming up again.

The first time: *For things left undome*.
The second time: *For things done*.
The third time: *For wrong intentions*.

Mutual Absolution    In silence, each in turn around the room, we make and receive the sign of the cross on each other's foreheads.

Peace    We greet each other in silence.

Dance    Time: $\frac{4}{4}$
With weight on right foot, left foot forward, left foot behind. Next, in the same step shift weight to the left foot and point right foot to the right, shift weight to right foot and point left foot to the left. Cross left foot in front of right foot three times.

Repeat whole dance three times, or more.

Eucharistic Prayer   Follow the gestures of the celebrant as you wish.

'The Lord be with you': extend your arms with the palms out and the fingertips upwards.

'Lift up your hearts': turn your palms towards the ceiling and raise your arms to just above head level.

'Let us give thanks': lower palms so that fingertips are extended away from the body.

'Holy, Holy, Holy': together raise your hands in the air and shake fingers as though they were bells.

Return to the position of 'Let us give thanks' with arms and palms raised and fingertips extended away from the body.

The blessing of the bread and wine: the celebrant holds the bread up, breaks it, and lifts the cup.

The Lord's Prayer: Spread arms sideways, with palms facing forwards and fingers pointing upwards. Bring arms together so that palms touch in a gesture of prayer at heart level.

The bread and wine is shared. After receiving communion, there are a few moments for final reflection and individual prayers.

Blessing   A bowl of water is placed in the centre of the circle. Come forward, dip a finger or two in the water, and bless someone with living water.

## Final Prayer

We do not understand, eternal God,
the ways of your Spirit in the lives
of women and men.
She comes along secret paths to
take us unawares.
She touches us in joy and sorrow
to make us whole.
She hides behind coincidence to
lead us forward and
uses our human accidents as occasions
for influence.
We do not understand but
we welcome her presence and
rejoice in her power.

## Index of
## First Lines

And our approach was in peace.................................................................61
As one who travels in the heat.................................................................46
As women bake bread and share it with their families.................................64

Be gentle when you touch bread.................................................................64
Be healed, be whole.................................................................60
Be in love with life.................................................................39
Be silent.................................................................39
Beloved, our Father and Mother.................................................................63
Bless the Lord, my soul.................................................................84
Broken for us.................................................................64
Brother/Sister, be at peace.................................................................61

Christ our healer.................................................................44
Christ, our only true light.................................................................45
Come, let us celebrate the supper of Jesus.................................................................65

Flame-dancing Spirit, come.................................................................44
For all the saints who from their labour rest.................................................................85
For the darkness of waiting.................................................................55
From the flowing of the tide.................................................................54
From the fragmented world of our everyday lives.................................................................38

Glory be to you.................................................................41
Glory in all my seeing.................................................................41
Glory to God, glory to God.................................................................42
God forgives you.................................................................60
God is with us.................................................................66
God makes peace within us.................................................................61
God of justice and peace, you stand with those who are poor.................................................................54
God of love and forgiveness.................................................................59
God of the outsider.................................................................43
God our deliverer.................................................................44
God our mother.................................................................45
God whose body is all creation.................................................................44
God you know us as we are.................................................................57

God, lover of us all, most holy one...................................................................................................63

God, who cares for us................................................................................................................63

I deny God's gifts in me.............................................................................................................57

I light the candle.......................................................................................................................53

I will pour clean water upon you................................................................................................59

In the beginning........................................................................................................................40

In the beginning was God..........................................................................................................56

In the beginning, God made the world........................................................................................50

Into your hands, Lord................................................................................................................54

Jesus, who was lost and found in the garden...............................................................................43

Jubilate Deo.............................................................................................................................84

Keeper and Companion of us all, forgive us................................................................................58

Let thy Resurrection light radiate all our worship.........................................................................45

Let us give thanks.....................................................................................................................76

Let us go out in peace and power...............................................................................................80

Loving God..............................................................................................................................40

May God be with you................................................................................................................68

May Holy Wisdom.....................................................................................................................81

May the God who dances in creation..........................................................................................81

May the power and the mystery go before us...............................................................................81

Now may every living being.......................................................................................................81

O Christ the Risen Word............................................................................................................45

O God our deliverer...................................................................................................................43

O God, I seek you while you may be found..................................................................................38

O God, our Father and our Mother..............................................................................................70

O God, the power of the powerless.............................................................................................43

O God, we bring you our failure.................................................................................................57

O Gracious God........................................................................................................................45

O living Bread from Heaven.......................................................................................................64

O Lord, hear my prayer.............................................................................................................84

Peace I leave with you......................................................................................61
Peace and love are always alive in us...............................................................61
Peace is flowing like a river.............................................................................61

Rage, Wisdom, and our lives inflame.................................................................83

Sisters and brothers of the Community of St Hilda...............................................53
Spirit of integrity..........................................................................................45
Spirit of Truth..............................................................................................44

Thanks be to God that we have risen this day.....................................................44
The blessing of God.......................................................................................81
The blessing of the God of Sarah and Hagar, as of Abraham..................................81
The bread we bring.......................................................................................62
The feast is ended; depart in peace..................................................................80
The Living God.............................................................................................39
The wilderness and the dry land shall be glad......................................................46
This, the springtime of the year.......................................................................82
Those who work for change suffer resistance.......................................................80
Today we share bread and wine together...........................................................65

Ubi caritas et amor.......................................................................................84

vige creatrix sophia.......................................................................................83

We adore the glory and the truth that is God.......................................................41
We believe in God, Maker, Redeemer and Sustainer of Life....................................51
We believe in God, who created women and men in God's own image.....................49
We believe in the presence of God in the world...................................................48
We come with offerings...................................................................................62
We do not understand, eternal God...................................................................89
We have come together in this quiet space..........................................................38
We hold up our smallness to your greatness........................................................62
We meet together to share this meal..................................................................61
We need your forgiveness, merciful God..............................................................57
We take bread..............................................................................................72
When people turn...........................................................................................80

When we break bread together..................................................................................................... 65

When the time was right, God sent the Son.............................................................................. 50

With bread and wine, the signs of God's passion..................................................................... 65

Woman/Man, your sins are forgiven............................................................................................ 60


You can't kill the spirit................................................................................................................84

You shall go out with joy.............................................................................................................84